A History of the United States
From Colony to Superpower

John A. Williams

INDEX

Introduction

A. The Book's Goals and Intents

The narrative that characterizes the United States of America is rich and complicated, and "A History of the United States: From Colony to Superpower" explores this richness and complexity in depth. This book is meant to give readers a comprehensive overview of the nation's development from its colonial era roots to its present day position as a worldwide superpower. This book covers a wide range of topics that have formed the American experience, including significant political, social, economic, and cultural shifts.

The book's overarching goal is to provide readers with a meticulously researched and interesting story that vividly depicts the major events and influential figures that have molded the United States. We hope that by looking at the nation's past we can better understand the forces that have contributed to its development, difficulties, and eventual triumphs. By doing so, readers can better understand the forces that shaped the United States into the nation it is today and the global power it wields.

To that end, the book is broken up into sections, or chapters, that each cover a certain time period or topic in history. These sections offer a historical and thematic foundation for learning about the United States. From the first European settlements and the American Revolution to the Civil War, the Gilded Age, the wars, the Civil Rights Movement, and modern America, readers will learn about it all. By looking at these various time periods, readers may see how America's ideals, institutions, and international ties have changed over time.

The book covers a wide swath of ground, touching on both familiar and underexplored topics in American history. It dives into the social and cultural aspects of American life as well as the important political and military events. This method provides a more all-encompassing view of the nation's development, difficulties, and resiliency. Topics that have had a significant influence in molding American culture and society, such as women's changing roles, race relations, economic shifts, and cultural upheavals, will be covered.

The author also acknowledges the connection between domestic and international issues. The United States' rise from colony to superpower was shaped by international alliances and wars as much as by domestic factors. Events including the two world wars, the cold war, and the decades after September 11th are examined in depth for their effect on the national identity and international standing of the United States. Understanding the United States' place in international history from this sweeping vantage point is illuminating.

"A History of the United States" aims to be read by as many people as possible. It's great for anyone looking to learn more about American history, whether they're a student, a teacher, or just a curious citizen. This book avoids using too much academic jargon, making it accessible to readers without broad historical backgrounds without sacrificing the level of analysis that will interest more seasoned readers.

To sum up, "A History of the United States: From Colony to Superpower" aims to provide an interesting and illuminating tour of American history, from its colonial beginnings to its current position as a world power. This book tries to give readers a full picture of the United States' history and its place in the globe by providing an all-encompassing narrative of the country's evolution and important events and dynamics. This book is an invitation to anyone interested in learning more about the intriguing and diverse story of the United States, be they students, teachers, or curious readers.

B. Importance of Understanding U.S. History

The study of U.S. history is vitally important for everyone, not just Americans. Knowledge of U.S. history is relevant regardless of when or where it is studied because it provides insight into the origins of a nation, the development of its principles, and the far-reaching consequences of its actions. Here are a few of the most persuasive arguments for studying U.S. history:

1. Cultural and National Identity: A broad understanding of U.S. history is vital to the development of American cultural and national identity. It's a way for people to feel a part of the nation's history, honor the sacrifices of the forefathers, and remain true to the principles that make America great. One's sense of community and national pride might grow via exposure to the stories of one's ancestors' sacrifices and triumphs.

Second, an educated populace is essential to a functional democracy. An understanding of U.S. history equips citizens to make educated judgments, contribute thoughtfully to public debates, and actively take part in the democratic process. It gives regular people the power to demand change from their government when it's not working.

3. Inspiration and Lessons There are many examples of perseverance, creativity, and advancement in American history. Learning from the struggles and successes of the past can help you find the strength to overcome the difficulties you're encountering right now. Furthermore, history teaches us important lessons regarding the results of our actions and the policies we've implemented.

4. Historical Context: Current events have deep roots in the past. Learning about the past helps provide light on the present, whether one is interested in politics, racial harmony, economic inequality, or international relations. By understanding the past, people are better able to navigate the present.

5. A World View: The United States has been a driving force in the development of international politics and events. To fully grasp the dynamics of international alliances and wars, a familiarity with U.S. history is required. It throws light on the U.S.'s role as a superpower, its foreign policy decisions, and its impact on the world stage.

The United States is a cultural and ethnic mosaic, and its history is shaped by the perspectives of its many different people groups. Awareness of other cultures and an appreciation for diversity are cultivated via education on the experiences and accomplishments of groups as diverse as Native Americans, African Americans, immigrants, and women.

7. Human Rights and Social Justice: Major struggles for civil rights and social justice have shaped the course of American history. The fights for civil rights and women's suffrage, among others, have opened the path for more fairness and development in society. For modern-day advocates of justice, an awareness of these struggles is essential.

8. Economic Knowledge: The United States' economic history is a living monument to the efficacy of creativity, initiative, and free market forces. Understanding economic cycles, policies, and the nation's strengths and weaknesses requires familiarity with this background.

9. Global Interconnectedness: As the world becomes more and more interconnected, the effects of an occurrence in one region of the world might have far-reaching effects elsewhere. Understanding the United States' past can help people see how their actions today affect other people throughout the world.

Keeping the past alive is important because it serves as a nation's collective memory. Learning about America's past is a great way to make sure its founders and influential citizens aren't forgotten. This preservation of memory acknowledges the sacrifices and achievements of former generations.

In conclusion, the value of learning U.S. history cannot be emphasized. To an international audience, it provides vital background and insights while also serving as a source of American identity, knowledge, and inspiration. Investigating the nation's past can shed light on how it has shaped the present and the future. It's crucial for creating more just and equitable communities and enlightened leaders.

C. Topics and Ideas That Shaped the United States' Past

The United States' rich and varied past is a complex tapestry of ideas and events that have influenced and formed the country. It is impossible to grasp the intricacy of U.S. history without first understanding these basic concepts. Here, we go into some of the defining ideas and concepts that have shaped the American story:

The pursuit of freedom and individual autonomy is central to the American experience. Many people have looked to the United States as a beacon of freedom, from those who fought for independence in the colonies, to those who championed individual rights and the end of slavery. A recurring theme in American history is the fight for equal rights and fair treatment of all people.

The conviction that it was America's divinely-appointed purpose to expand its territory over the North American continent is at the heart of the concept of Manifest Destiny. This ideology pushed westward expansion, the Oregon Trail, and the annexation of Texas, among other developments. It also stoked tensions with the indigenous peoples of the Americas and Mexico.

The United States is frequently referred to as a "nation of immigrants," and this diversity is a major reason why. The history of immigration has increased the country's cultural tapestry and economic power. This is a tale of optimism, possibility, and, unfortunately, discrimination and prejudice. Both the "melting pot" and the "salad bowl" metaphors, which are relatively new, represent America's multicultural makeup.

The United States is a democracy, and its history is distinguished by the fight for independence from a centralized government. Democracies and the rule of law have been exemplified throughout American history by events like the American Revolution, the Constitutional Convention, and the ongoing discussions about how much authority the federal government should have compared to the states.

Slavery and the fight for equal rights are two of the most significant events in American history. The moral and political evolution of the country was influenced by the institution of slavery, its abolition, and the civil rights campaigns for African Americans and other disenfranchised groups. Symbolic of these fights are historical heroes like Frederick Douglass, Harriet Tubman, and Martin Luther King, Jr.

Sixthly, Industrialization and Innovation: The United States has long led the way in these areas. Economic expansion and increased urbanization resulted from the effects of the industrial revolution. Technological progress in the world would not have been possible without the contributions of innovators like Thomas Edison, Henry Ford, and Steve Jobs.

U.S. policy toward the rest of the world has swung between isolationism and internationalism throughout its history. The United States has gone between periods of isolationism, epitomized by the Monroe Doctrine, and internationalism, as evidenced by its involvement in both World Wars and its position of leadership within the United Nations.

8. Economic Growth and Inequality: Economic expansion has been a constant in the United States' story, from the market revolution of the 19th century to the tech boom of the 20th and 21st. However, income disparity has frequently followed economic progress, sparking discussions about fairness in the allocation of wealth.

The importance of the environment to the American people is emphasized in number nine. Growing environmental consciousness is reflected in measures like the protection of natural areas and the creation of national parks. Key figures in this field include Theodore Roosevelt.

10. Global Superpower: The United States became a major player in international politics, economy, and culture during the 20th century. This topic covers everything from the Cold War to the armaments race to the space race to the effect of U.S. foreign policy on international relations.

The fight for gender equality has been a recurring subject in American history, which brings us to topic number eleven: Gender and Women's Rights. The fight for women's suffrage, the rise of the feminist movement, and the breaking of barriers for women in a variety of sectors are all crucial to comprehending the country's development.

12. Tension Between Individualism and Community: While American culture celebrates independence and autonomy, it also places a premium on belonging and working together. The struggle between personal freedoms and collective responsibilities is a perennial one in American history.

Appreciating the complexities, contradictions, and successes that have created the American experience requires an understanding of these fundamental themes and concepts in U.S. history. These motifs allow us to examine the nation's history and its lasting effects on the present and the future. People and cultures all throughout the world can find something to identify with in the rich fabric that is American history.

Chapter 1: The Colonial Era (1607-1776)

1.1 Early European Settlements

Exploration, colonization, and the intricate interactions between the Old World and the New World characterize the story of the earliest European settlements in North America, a seminal period in American history. These communities shaped the future of the United States and had far-reaching effects on native peoples and the flow of history.

In 1492, Christopher Columbus sailed to the Caribbean under the flag of Spain, marking the beginning of the age of European discovery and colonization. A new era of exploration and conquering has begun with this journey. Portugal, England, France, and the Netherlands were just a few of the European superpowers that followed Spain and Italy in exploring the Americas.

Examples of early European colonies in the territory that would become the United States are:

It was the Spanish explorers that first settled the southern regions of North America. Florida was discovered and claimed by Spain in 1513 thanks to the efforts of Juan Ponce de León. St. Augustine, Florida, was founded by the Spanish in 1565 and is the oldest European town in the continental United States. Missions were also founded in cities across the American Southwest by the Spanish.

Two, the English Colonies were founded in 1607 when the English established a colony at Jamestown, Virginia. The colonization of North America by the English officially began at this time. The colony was established by the Virginia Company, which saw opportunity in the region's tobacco. Jamestown endured and prospered despite numerous challenges, like as hostilities with native peoples, sickness, and poor living circumstances.

In 1620, a group of religious dissenters known as the Pilgrims sailed on the Mayflower and established Plymouth Colony in what is now the state of Massachusetts. The Mayflower Compact was their attempt at self-government and religious freedom. As a symbol of the cooperation and shared traditions between the English settlers and the indigenous Wampanoag people, their narrative is frequently linked to the first Thanksgiving.

New Netherland, which encompassed sections of modern-day New York, New Jersey, Delaware, and Connecticut, was founded by the Dutch in the early 17th century. New Amsterdam, near the end of Manhattan, flourished as a trading post because that was the primary focus of the Dutch. The Dutch colony of New Netherland was conquered by the English in 1664, and the city was renamed New York.

5. French Colonies: The French explored and founded colonies throughout the Mississippi River Valley and the Great Lakes region, including Quebec in Canada. They set up a series of forts and trading posts and began engaging in the fur trade. Cities founded by the French, such as Detroit and New Orleans, left an indelible mark on the local language and culture.

There were a lot of good and bad things for the first European settlers to encounter in North America. Cooperation and trade were hallmarks of some encounters between European settlers and native populations, whereas conflict, displacement, and violence were more common in other encounters. Economic factors, such as the quest for new markets, trading routes, and precious resources, often prompted these communities to form.

The initial European colonies also paved the way for the formation of geographically and culturally separate sub-national entities. A variety of economic, social, and political systems emerged across the colonies, from those in New England and the Chesapeake Bay area to those in the Middle Colonies and the Southern Colonies.

The tension between competing cultures and economic interests would only increase as these communities grew. The French and Indian War and the Anglo-Powhatan Wars were just the beginning of a string of battles that began with territorial disputes and continued because of cultural and religious differences. These efforts would pave the way for the American Revolution and the eventual establishment of the United States, as well as alter the course of North American colonial history.

In sum, the era of first European colonization in North America is often considered to be the cornerstone of American history. Exploration, colonization, and the intricate connections between European settlers and native peoples all left their mark on these communities. These colonies play a vital role in American history because their legacies continue to shape the country's social, political, and cultural landscapes.

1.2 American identity can be traced back to the original 13 colonies.

The Thirteen Colonies constitute a significant and formative period in the history of the United States. In the 17th and 18th centuries, European powers created settlements across the Americas. These communities were crucial in the formation of the new nation, the formation of its identity, and the establishment of key concepts that would come to define the United States.

Each of the Thirteen Colonies had its own history, culture, and traits that marked it apart from the others. New England, the Middle Colonies, and the Southern Colonies are the three major groups that make up the colonies.

The New England Colonies (Massachusetts, New Hampshire, Connecticut, and Rhode Island) were founded on a foundation of Puritan theological tenets. In their quest for religious autonomy and independence from the Church of England, the Puritans founded close-knit communities where education and local leadership were prioritized. The Pilgrims' dedication to independence and education is exemplified by the Mayflower Compact and the establishment of Harvard University in 1636. New England's economy based on fishing, shipbuilding, trading, and subsistence farming.

The Middle Colonies, which included the states of New York, New Jersey, Pennsylvania, and Delaware, had a more varied population of different races and religions. New York's Dutch heritage and Pennsylvania's Quaker settlements fostered an atmosphere of religious acceptance. The rich soil in the middle colonies made them ideal for farming, commerce, and trade. In particular, Philadelphia became a center of political and intellectual life, making important contributions to the rise of the American Enlightenment and the establishment of democratic ideals.

Thirdly, the Southern Colonies had an agrarian economy based on big estates and cash crops like tobacco and rice. This region included the states of Virginia, Maryland, North Carolina, South Carolina, and Georgia. A distinctive Southern culture and social order developed as a result of the plantation system's reliance on enslaved labor. The growth of the plantation economy and the continuation of slavery would have far-reaching effects on the nation's development.

Despite regional differences, the Thirteen Colonies had many things in common that helped forge a national identity:

First, the concept of Self-Government emerged in several of the colonies and has since become deeply rooted in the fabric of American democratic heritage. Early instances of colonial assemblies that lay the groundwork for representative governance include the Mayflower Compact, the Fundamental Orders of Connecticut, and the House of Burgesses in Virginia.

2. Religious Freedom: Many religious dissenters from Europe fled to the colonies in search of religious freedom. Later on, the separation of religion and state and the guarantee of religious freedom would come to define the American character.

Thirdly, Cultural Exchange: The colonists' varied cultural and ethnic backgrounds shaped American civilization and led to its eventual acceptance of variety. This included the English, Dutch, French, Spanish, and African peoples.

Having achieved economic self-sufficiency, the colonies gained a sense of autonomy from European rulers. The United States' economic basis was laid by trade and commerce between the colonies and with other countries.

5. Conflict and Cooperation: The colonies faced different problems, including confrontations with Native American groups, border issues, and external threats. Diplomatic and military expertise were crucial during the American Revolution and the early years of the nation, and the capacity to negotiate these obstacles, whether through alliances or battles, contributed to their development.

In the United States' constitutional documents, the Thirteen Colonies' contributions are memorialized. The Declaration of Independence, the United States Constitution, and the Bill of Rights owe a great debt to the concepts of liberty, self-governance, and religious freedom that arose throughout the colonial era.

Overall, the first 13 colonies were crucial in shaping the character and culture of the United States. The United States would not be what it is today without the contributions of people from all walks of life. These early American settlements laid the groundwork for the ideals of individual liberty, religious toleration, and cross-cultural interaction that continue to inform the fabric of modern America. The Thirteen Colonies are a symbol of the past's continuing influence on America's present and future.

1.3 The Encounter and Conflict with Native Americans: A Complex History.

The interactions between European colonists and indigenous peoples in North America are a tragic and nuanced chapter in the continent's history. The encounter between these two diverse worlds, each with its own cultures, traditions, and worldviews, would have far-reaching effects that continue to affect the United States and the Native American experience to this day.

Native American Cultures Before European Contact:
Native Americans in North America spoke dozens of different languages and practiced hundreds of different customs before Europeans arrived. These civilizations varied greatly, from the nomadic Plains tribes to the agricultural Eastern Woodlands towns to the sophisticated societies of the Southwestern United States.

"First Encounters"
Curiosity and commerce characterized the early encounters between Native Americans and European explorers. Native Americans helped early Europeans in the New World by providing food, agricultural practices, and geographical information. In exchange, they were met with a slew of unfamiliar inventions, commodities, and diseases.

Disease's Repercussions:
The introduction of communicable diseases to which Native Americans had no protection, such as smallpox, measles, and influenza, was one of the most catastrophic results of European contact. The devastating death toll and social upheaval caused by these diseases wiped out entire indigenous populations.

Tensions emerged when European colonies spread for reasons including competition for natural resources and cultural differences. As tensions rose, other wars and conflicts sprang out. Native American groups occasionally banded together or formed alliances with European states in an effort to safeguard their own interests.

Dispossession of Native American territory was a common consequence of European colonialism in North America. Accompanying this movement were land treaties and land cessions, many of which involved some form of duress, deception, or blatant robbery. There were significant cultural, economic, and social effects of the forced relocation of indigenous people to reserves.

Trade's Crucial Function:
Early interactions between Native Americans and Europeans revolved largely around commercial exchanges. Native Americans were skilled merchants who traded furs, pelts, and agricultural supplies for metal equipment, weapons, and fabrics imported from Europe. This commerce promoted economic interconnectedness but also led to exploitation and reliance, which were both negative outcomes.

The Treaty System
Treaties were negotiated between the federal government and indigenous communities throughout American history. The purpose of these agreements was to set ground rules for sharing territory and settling disputes. However, numerous treaties were broken, which resulted in even more territory being lost and more wars.

Relocations and Displacements Caused by Force:
The forced removal of numerous Native American tribes is one of the darkest chapters in the history of U.S. relations with indigenous peoples. A well-known example is the Indian Removal Act of 1830, which ultimately resulted in the Trail of Tears for the Cherokee Nation. These forceful removals resulted in the deaths of thousands of Native Americans.

Cultural assimilation and repression

The United States government adopted measures with the intention of integrating indigenous people into mainstream American society. Many Native American children were forcibly removed from their homes and sent to boarding schools, where they were generally denied access to their cultural and linguistic heritage.

The Power of Struggle and Perseverance:

Native American societies, although facing innumerable obstacles, have shown to be remarkably resilient and resistant. The preservation of indigenous traditions and the assertion of the rights of Native nations have benefited greatly from cultural revival, land reclamation, and tribal sovereignty movements.

Native Americans still deal with issues like poverty, health inequities, lack of education opportunities, and territorial disputes in the present day. These challenges underline the ongoing battle for self-determination and the safeguarding of Native rights.

Relations between European settlers and indigenous peoples in North America are a complicated and multidimensional part of the continent's history. This is a history full of triumph and tragedy, resiliency and catastrophe, cultural exchange and oppression. The continuous efforts to protect indigenous cultures and rights, as well as the social, political, and economic issues faced by Native American communities today, are all clear manifestations of the lingering legacies of these interactions. Recognizing the lasting effects of these interactions and working for a more just and inclusive future for all requires an appreciation of this past.

1.4 The American Revolution: The Birth of a Nation

The American Revolution, a major event in world history, was a struggle for independence and self-determination that ultimately resulted in the establishment of the United States of America. From 1775 to 1783, a remarkable historical event occurred that would alter the political, social, and cultural landscape of North America for all time.

Reasons for the American Revolution:
Years of resentment and frustration built up to a boiling point during the American Revolution. Essential elements included:

First, the American colonies were subjected to "Taxation without Representation," in which the British government imposed various levies (such as the Stamp Act and the Tea Act) on them without their approval. Colonists in the Americas sang "no taxation without representation" as a rallying cry.

2. British Colonial Policies: British efforts to tighten control over the colonies and enforce trade rules, such as the Navigation Acts, were greeted with resistance. More and more colonists saw these regulations as repressive.

Conflicts and demonstrations, such as the Boston Massacre and the Boston Tea Party, ratcheted up the temperature. In April 1775, at the Battles of Lexington and Concord, the first shots of the Revolution were fired.

Independence Proclamation:
The Declaration of Independence, published on July 4, 1776, was a watershed moment in the Revolution. Thomas Jefferson's primary work, the Declaration of Independence, announced the colonies' desire for independence from British rule. It defined American ideals like freedom, equality before the law, and the right to life, liberty, and the pursuit of happiness.

The War of Independence:
A prolonged war between the American colonies and the British Empire sprang out of the initial American Revolution. Bunker Hill, Saratoga, and Yorktown were only a few of the famous conflicts fought there. France provided critical aid to the American soldiers led by George Washington, which was instrumental in their triumph over the British.

Important People During the Revolution:

1. George Washington: As the commander-in-chief of the Continental Army, Washington's leadership was vital in securing American freedom. His resolve and determination were an example to his men and to the country.

To secure French support for the American cause, the Americans relied heavily on diplomat, philosopher, and inventor Benjamin Franklin.

Third, Thomas Jefferson, whose elegant language in the Declaration of Independence encapsulated the ideals and aspirations of the colonies.

"John Adams" (No. 4): Adams was a key figure in the Continental Congress and the establishment of diplomatic relations with other countries because of his fervent support for independence.

Five, the French aristocrat and military leader known as the Marquis de Lafayette, who was instrumental in the American victory at Yorktown.

Revolution's Aftermath:
The ripple effects of the American Revolution were felt far beyond North America.

First, the Constitutional Convention: The Revolutionary War officially ended with the Treaty of Paris in 1783, which established the United States as a sovereign nation. It laid the groundwork for the new republic.

Second, the Revolution's ideas, like as natural rights and popular sovereignty, influenced movements for independence and self-determination all over the world.

Thirdly, the United States Constitution was written in 1787 as a result of the Revolution and established the basis for the American system of government and its ideas of checks and balances, federalism, and individual rights.

The Revolution sparked debates about the proper role of government and the expansion of political rights, which led to point number four on this list, Expanding Democracy. It was a pivotal moment in the evolution of American political institutions and the expansion of voting rights.

5. Ongoing Struggles: The Revolution did not end all prejudice and inequity, especially against African Americans and Native Americans. These problems would remain and change over the years.

The American Revolution's Lasting Impact
The American Revolution left behind an enduring symbol of the strength of a people's will to achieve independence and freedom. The Revolution's ideals continue to define American culture and the country's place in the world. The Revolution forged the United States into a nation dedicated to freedom, democracy, and the pursuit of happiness. This dedication to these ideas is a defining characteristic of the United States today.

Chapter 2: The Early Republic (1776-1824)

2.1 Revolution and Compromise: The Birth of the United States

Amazing and turbulent, the path to the United States was paved with revolutionary zeal, political ingenuity, and difficult compromises. The late 18th century saw the beginning of a process of nation-building that would lead to the formation of a unified and independent nation that would go on to become one of the world's most influential democracies.

Context and Colonial Unrest:
By the middle of the 18th century, nearly two centuries had passed since the British had gained control of the American colonies. The colonists established a distinct American identity during this time while keeping close ties to the mother country of Britain. This connection, however, was gradually weakened by a number of disagreements and arguments.

Taxation and Civil Disobedience:
A series of taxes imposed by the British government on the American colonies without their approval stoked the flames of discontent. The Stamp Act and the Tea Act inflamed colonists' resentment because they felt they were being subjected to "taxation without representation."

The Ignition of Revolution:
The first military struggle between American colonists and British forces culminated in 1775 with the Battles of Lexington and Concord. This sparked revolutionary fervor and ultimately led to the formation of the Continental Congress in Philadelphia.

Independence Proclamation:
As of July 1776, the Declaration of Independence had been approved by the Continental Congress. Thomas Jefferson was the primary author of this declaration of independence from Great Britain that also set forth the ideals of personal freedom and representative democracy. On July 4, the

United States commemorates the day the Declaration of Independence was signed.

The War of Independence:
The American Revolution morphed into an all-out civil war. General George Washington's Continental Army engaged the British in a drawn-out war. British forces were ultimately defeated thanks to decisive French backing and key victories such as Saratoga and Yorktown.

An Overview of the Treaty of Paris (1783)
In 1783, the United States formally ended the Revolutionary War with the Treaty of Paris. This treaty established the United States as a sovereign nation and established its present-day geographical boundaries. The original colonies of the British Empire became the independent nation of the United States of America.

The Importance of Coming to Terms
It took not only revolutionary zeal but also careful negotiations to forge the United States. Several crucial agreements shaped the country:

One of the biggest obstacles the Philadelphia Convention of 1787 faced was how to fairly allocate seats in the new administration. The Great Compromise created a two-house legislature, with each state having an equal number of senators and representatives in the House of Representatives depending on population.

During the Constitutional Convention, delegates debated how to address slavery. This debate resulted in the Three-Fifths Compromise. To address concerns about underrepresentation for southern states, the agreement regarded enslaved individuals as three-fifths of a person for the purposes of representation.

Third, the Commerce Compromise ended debates in Congress about who had the power to oversee trade policies. The federal government was given jurisdiction over international and interstate business, while state governments were given authority over commercial activity inside their borders.

4. The Bill of Rights: A promise to include a Bill of Rights to defend individual freedoms was made in order to achieve passage of the new United States Constitution. Ten of the original amendments to the Constitution make up the Bill of Rights, which was ratified in 1791.

[The United States Constitution]
The United States Constitution, which established a federal system of government with checks and balances, was drafted at the 1787 Constitutional Convention. The stability and longevity of the nation can be directly attributed to the ideas of limited government, separation of powers, and individual liberties enshrined in the Constitution.

First President George Washington:
Known as the "Father of His Country," George Washington was chosen as the first President of the United States with 100% of the vote in 1789. The tone of the new nation was defined by his leadership and dedication to republican values.

A Fresh Start:
The foundation of the United States signified a fresh beginning, not only for the American colonies but for the world. When compared to the monarchies and authoritarian regimes that had hitherto dominated international affairs, the American experiment in self-governance constituted a radical departure.

The United States were formed as a result of political foresight, compromise, and the insatiable human thirst for independence and freedom. As a result, a nation was established on the basis of democratic principles and individual rights, becoming a model for people all over the world who aspire to be free and determine their own futures. As it faces new problems and seizes new possibilities, the United States remains true to its foundational values and its historical roots.

2.2 American democracy's foundational documents, the Constitution and Bill of Rights.

The Constitution and the Bill of Rights are cornerstones in American history because of the role they play in establishing the framework for government and protecting citizens' rights. Both the Declaration of Independence and the Constitution, written in the late 18th century, are still vital to the American political system because they guarantee that the values of freedom, equality, and democracy are at its foundation.

The Constitution of the United States as a Governing Document:
The United States Constitution is the highest law of the land. It was drafted during the Constitutional Convention in Philadelphia in 1787 and approved in 1788. Establishing the separation of powers and a system of checks and balances to prevent the concentration of power, it lays out the foundation for the federal government.

Important aspects of the American Constitution are:

One of the first things you'll notice about the Constitution is the Preamble, which lays out the overarching goals of the government. These goals include creating justice, advancing the general good, and securing the blessings of liberty for future generations.

 In this section, the roles and responsibilities of the Senate and House of Representatives in the United States government are laid forth. It lays out the rules for passing laws, collecting taxes, and calling for military action.

Article 2 establishes the Executive Branch of government and defines the President's role as Chief Executive and Commander in Chief of the Armed Forces.

Article III established the federal judiciary, with the Supreme Court as its head, and lays out the scope of jurisdiction for federal courts.

Article IV, "The States," details the federal government's relationship with the states, including the Full Faith and Credit Clause, the Privileges and Immunities Clause, and the procedure for admitting new states to the Union.

Article V, "Amendments," allows the Constitution to be updated to reflect new circumstances and societal norms. It requires a two-thirds majority in Congress or a convention called for by two-thirds of state legislatures to propose an amendment, with ratification by three-fourths of the states.

Article VI, the "Supremacy Clause," declares the Constitution to be the highest law of the land and mandates that all courts uphold it regardless of any conflicting state laws or constitutions.

To ratify the Constitution, nine of the original thirteen states had to give their consent, as described in Article VII.

Individual Freedoms Guaranteed under the Bill of Rights:
The Bill of Rights, the first 10 amendments to the Constitution, were added in 1791 in response to growing concerns about the security of citizens' fundamental liberties. These amendments protect the rights and freedoms of the American people and act as a shield against tyranny on the part of the government.

Some of the most important parts of the Bill of Rights are:

The First Amendment protects the rights to free speech, religion, press, assembly, and petition for all U.S. citizens.

The Second Amendment ensures citizens' right to keep and bear weapons, legalizing the possession and use of firearms by private citizens.

The Third Amendment forbids the unauthorized quartering of troops in private houses during times of peace.

The Fourth Amendment to the United States Constitution prohibits the use of warrantless searches and seizures by government officials.

The Fifth Amendment guarantees fair trials, prevents double jeopardy, and makes it illegal to incriminate oneself.

The Sixth Amendment guarantees a person a public trial, access to counsel, and the opportunity to cross-examine prosecution witnesses.

The right to a jury trial in civil proceedings is protected by the Seventh Amendment.

The Eighth Amendment outlaws high bail and fees in addition to cruel and unusual punishment.

The Ninth Amendment ensures that the people's additional rights not specifically included in the Constitution are protected from being interpreted away.

The Tenth Amendment provides that the federal government does not have the authority to do anything that has not been specifically given to it by the states or the people.

The Long-Term Effects:
The Constitution and the Bill of Rights are still very influential on modern American politics and culture. The courts have interpreted and reinterpreted them, allowing them to adapt to the nation's evolving requirements. They allow people to hold their government to account and ensure that everyone has equal access to the law and basic freedoms.

People all throughout the world, not only in the United States, look to these writings for guidance as they fight for democratic government and the protection of individual rights. Preserving the enduring heritage of the Founding Fathers and their goal for a more perfect union, the Constitution and the Bill of Rights continue to guide the nation as it navigates the complexities and challenges of the 21st century.

2.3 The Founding Fathers: The Men Who Built Our Democratic System in the United States

The Founding Fathers of the United States were extraordinary individuals who were instrumental in shaping the young nation. They helped form the intellectual, legal, and political ideas upon which the American system of government is based. In the midst of revolutionary upheaval, these men laid the groundwork for a new nation that would stand as a shining example of democracy, freedom, and individual rights.

The Forerunners:
The Founding Fathers were more than simply politicians; they were also visionaries who dared to think outside the box and create a new system of governance. Reason, individual rights, and the social compact were all central to Enlightenment philosophy, which many of them found inspirational. Their ideal nation would be one in which people were safe from tyranny and oppression and where the government got its power only from the people.

1. George Washington: Known as the "Father of His Country," Washington was the first President of the United States and a military hero during the American Revolutionary War. His example as president and as a person influenced future presidents.

Thomas Jefferson, the primary author of the Declaration of Independence, was a staunch supporter of personal liberty and the separation of church and state. He was the country's third head of state.

John Adams, the third on our list, was the second President of the United States and a staunch supporter of independence who played a key part in authoring the Declaration of Independence.

4. Benjamin Franklin: A polymath and diplomat, Franklin is best known for his work with electricity and his many published works on a wide range of topics. During the Revolutionary War, he played a pivotal role in winning over the French.

5. James Madison: Madison, who is often referred to as the "Father of the Constitution," was instrumental in the creation of both the United States Constitution and the Bill of Rights. The United States' fourth president, his presidency began after his death.

In addition to being a Federalist and the first Secretary of the Treasury, Alexander Hamilton also advocated for a powerful central government and a stable financial system. The United States Mint and the first national bank were both set up with his help.

John Jay, the first Chief Justice of the Supreme Court and a diplomat who wrote in the Federalist Papers, negotiated the Treaty of Paris that concluded the Revolutionary War.

8. Thomas Paine: Though not a Founding Father in the traditional sense, Paine's treatise "Common Sense" had a vital influence in rousing support for independence. To boost morale among American troops, he wrote "The American Crisis" series.

This is what they've given us:
The legacies of the Founding Fathers to the United States are manifold and everlasting:

First, Thomas Jefferson's Declaration of Independence, which encapsulates the conceptual foundations of American democracy. It asserted the independence of the colonies from British control and the rights of all people.

Many of the Founding Fathers met in 1787 for the Constitutional Convention, where they drafted the United States Constitution. Through meticulous drafting, James Madison established a system of federalism, separation of powers, and checks and balances for the federal government.

A commitment to include a Bill of Rights in the Constitution was made to secure its ratification. Freedom of expression, religion, and a fair trial are only few of the individual liberties safeguarded by the first 10 amendments, authored by James Madison and approved in 1791.

4. The Federalist Papers, a collection of essays written by Alexander Hamilton, James Madison, and John Jay, presented a persuasive argument for the ratification of the Constitution by outlining the document's benefits and rebutting common criticisms.

5. Foreign Relations: Benjamin Franklin and John Jay, two early American diplomats, negotiated international treaties that were instrumental in gaining French backing during the Revolutionary War.

Legacy Forever:
This country would not be what it is today without the contributions of the Founding Fathers. Individual rights, freedom, and the consent of the governed, among other concepts they outlined in the Declaration of Independence and the Constitution, are central to American identity and governance to this day.

Freedom, democracy, and the rule of law are all tenets of American society that the Founding Fathers helped establish. Not only Americans, but people all around the world who are working to create more just and equal communities look to their foresight, wisdom, and commitment to the ideas of liberty and self-governance for inspiration. The Founding Fathers' achievements are a demonstration of the long-lasting impact of ideas and the potential of individuals to shape the future in their own image.

2.4 Expansion and Development: Creating a New Nation in America

The history of the United States is inextricably connected with the idea of development and expansion, which reflects a never-ending zeal to discover, colonize, and develop uncharted territories. The United States underwent dramatic changes and played a pivotal role on the international scene from the earliest days of European colonization through the westward expansion, industrialization, and worldwide impact of the 19th and 20th centuries.

European settlers arrived in the Americas in the early 17th century, marking the beginning of a period of rapid development and expansion. English, French, Spanish, and Dutch colonists founded cities and colonies all along the Atlantic coast. These pioneers risked everything for the promise of a better life, including the freedom to practice their religion and the chance to start a new chapter in their lives.

Expansion to the West:
The westward expansion of the United States is a distinguishing characteristic of the country's history. A persistent trek across the continent was prompted by people looking for land, resources, and a better life. In 1803, the United States undertook the massive Lewis and Clark Expedition to explore and survey the recently acquired Louisiana Territory.

Destiny of the Manifest:
During the 19th century, the idea of "Manifest Destiny" emerged as a driving force. John O'Sullivan, a journalist, used the phrase in 1845 to describe the widespread conviction that the United States was tasked by God with extending its territory westward in order to preach democracy and the principles of individual freedom. This theory provided justification for the conquest and annexation of new territories, including those in the Southwest, California, and the Pacific Northwest; the Oregon Trail; the Mexican-American War; and Texas.

Industrialization's Repercussions

Industrialization was a major factor in the dramatic shifts of the nineteenth century. The country's economy and social structure were revolutionized by technological advances in transportation, communication, and technology. When the Transcontinental Railroad was finally finished in 1869, it represented the expanding influence and interconnectedness of the United States.

The Acquistion of Louisiana:

The Louisiana Purchase of 1803 was one of the most important land acquisitions in American history. After President Thomas Jefferson bought it from the French, the United States doubled in size and had plenty of room to grow to the west.

The Great Westward Migration, Including the Oregon Trail:

The roughly 2,000-mile journey from Missouri to Oregon on the Oregon Trail became a metaphor for the westward expansion of the United States in the mid-19th century. Thousands of pioneers and settlers took this path to the lush regions of the Oregon Territory in search of fresh chances, adventure, and a better life.

An Overview of the Mexican-American War

California, Arizona, and New Mexico were only some of the huge swaths of the American Southwest that were won from Mexico in the Mexican-American War (1846–1848). The battle and territorial conquests posed fresh problems concerning slavery and the rights of newly gained territories, but they also brought up new economic prospects in those regions.

Expansion of Slavery Into New Areas:

Slavery was a major factor in discussions over where to expand the nation's borders. Tensions over the growth of slavery led to the American Civil War in 1861, despite attempts to address the issue through the Missouri Compromise of 1820 and the Compromise of 1850.

The United States' Position in the World:
The United States' influence had spread outside North America by the late 19th and early 20th centuries. Following the Spanish-American War, it actively pursued overseas territorial acquisitions, including the annexation of Hawaii, the Philippines, and Guam. The United States became an influential actor in world politics and wars.

Conclusion:
Expansion and development have played essential roles in American history and identity. Once a loose confederation of Atlantic coast colonies, the United States is now a continental powerhouse. The idea of Manifest Destiny, the thirst for gold, and the pioneering spirit all drove the United States westward.

However, the story of development and expansion is also distinguished by complicated and often distressing issues, such as the extermination and mistreatment of native peoples, wars with other countries, and the persistence of slavery and racial discrimination. It's an inspiring and challenging tale that has shaped and will continue to shape American ideals and principles.

The United States is still trying to figure out how to grow and expand in terms of immigration, environmental protection, and international power. Powered by an unwavering faith in the promise of the American Dream and the possibility of a greater future, the United States of America uses the lessons of its past, with its successes and struggles, to navigate the complexities of the 21st century.

Chapter 3: Westward Expansion and the Age of Jackson (1824-1848)

3.1 The ideology of American westward expansion known as "Manifest Destiny."

In the 19th century, the concept of Manifest Destiny was widely held and served as a guiding principle for American westward development. They believed it was their patriotic duty to populate the entirety of the North American continent with their brand of democracy, industry, and devotion to individual freedom. This idea influenced the development of the United States and had far-reaching effects on the native populations of the area.

Where Did Manifest Destiny Come From?
Journalist John L. O'Sullivan originally used the term "Manifest Destiny" in an article supporting Texas's annexation in 1845. According to O'Sullivan, it is America's "manifest destiny to overspread the continent allotted by Providence for the free development of our yearly multiplying millions." This term embodied the conviction that the United States had a divine purpose to advance westward.

Manifest Destiny's Most Important Components

First, Continental Expansion: According to Manifest Destiny, the United States was destined to grow to encompass the entire North American continent, from the Atlantic to the Pacific.

Proponents of Manifest Destiny felt that the superiority of American civilization and democratic values warranted their export to uncharted regions. This was seen as a means to spread civilization and enlightenment to less developed regions.

Access to lucrative resources, fertile land, and markets for American goods were all considered as potential benefits of expanding America's territory.

Security and Defense 4. Some advocates suggested that expansion would provide strategic advantages and buffer zones against potential foreign attacks.

Application of Manifest Destiny to Westward Expansion: Major Turning Points in American History

One of the most visible signs of the United States' westward growth was the Louisiana Purchase (1803), in which the country acquired the huge Louisiana Territory, effectively doubling its size.

Symbolizing the westward movement spurred by Manifest Destiny was the Oregon Trail, which pioneers used in the middle of the 19th century to colonize the Oregon Territory.

Third, in The Annexation of Texas (1845), Texas was officially added to the United States after a period of tension with Mexico that was stoked by the presence of American settlers in what was then Mexican territory.

The concept in Manifest Destiny was a major factor in the United States' decision to go to war with Mexico during the Mexican-American War (1846-1848). Due to the war, the states of California and New Mexico were added to the United States' possessions.

5 The California Gold Rush (1848): The finding of gold in California attracted a tremendous flood of people, reinforcing the idea of westward expansion as a method to reach affluence.

In 1846, the United States and Great Britain signed the Oregon Treaty, which permanently fixed the international boundary between the two countries at the 49th parallel and ended a decades-long territorial dispute.

Significant Challenges and Controversies: Manifest Destiny, while propelling westward growth, also brought about:

1. The Displacement of Native Americans: The westward expansion caused the uprooting and dispossessed of native populations. American colonizers encroached on Native American lands, causing Native Americans to lose their homes and way of life.

Second, slavery became a divisive topic when it was introduced to the newly conquered regions. The controversy over whether these regions would tolerate slavery or not heightened sectional tensions, eventually contributing to the American Civil War.

Thirdly, the Environmental Impact of the Westward Expansion was substantial, resulting in things like the exhaustion of natural resources, the cutting down of trees, and the alteration of ecosystems.

International Conflicts: The United States became involved in the Mexican-American War and border disputes with Canada because of Manifest Destiny.

The Lasting Impact of Manifest Fate:

The philosophy made it possible for the country to realize its dream of expanding from sea to shining sea by acquiring huge new territory.

2. National Identity: It helped shape a distinctively American sense of who we are as a people, one that is based on the ideal of America as a land-expanding, forward-thinking pioneer.

While it paved the way for great progress and new opportunities for many, it did so at the price of indigenous peoples and prompted serious moral and ethical concerns.

These days, we look back at Manifest Destiny with a critical eye, weighing its merits and detriments. It's a historical artifact that shows how difficult it was for the country to balance its past commitments to democracy and fairness with the realities of westward expansion and cultural conflict.

3.2 The Trail of Tears is Native American History's Darkest Chapter.

Native Americans have long remembered the Trail of Tears as a terrible turning point in their interactions with the federal government of the United States. This forcible relocation, beginning by the Indian Removal Act of 1830, resulted in the misery and death of thousands of indigenous people as they were forcibly transported from their native lands in the southeastern United States.

Background:
Cherokee, Creek, Choctaw, Chickasaw, and Seminole were just few of the indigenous peoples who called the southeastern United States home before Europeans arrived. These countries developed sophisticated agricultural techniques, administrative systems, and cultural traditions over time.

The government of the United States became more envious of the rich farmland occupied by these native peoples in the early 19th century, especially that of the Cherokee in Georgia. After the discovery of gold in Cherokee territory, white immigrants arrived hoping to develop the area's agricultural potential.

The 1830 Indian Appropriation Act:
Andrew Jackson signed the Indian Removal Act into law after it was enacted by Congress in 1830. This law gave the federal government the green light to negotiate land swap treaties with Native American tribes, particularly in present-day Oklahoma, from the southeastern states in exchange for territory west of the Mississippi River.

Native American Opposition:
Some native communities accepted removal treaties, but many others fought them. Principal Chief John Ross and the rest of the Cherokee nation resisted Georgia's attempts to assert its control over their land and did not sign a removal treaty. In the 1832 case Worcester v. Georgia, the Supreme Court of the United States sided with the Cherokee and recognized their right to self-government. However, President Jackson

notoriously disregarded the order, reportedly declaring, "John Marshall has made his decision; now let him enforce it."

Forcible Displacement
Under General Winfield Scott's leadership, the United States government began the forcible relocation of the Cherokee in 1838. Nearly 4,000 Cherokee people lost their lives to famine, exposure, and other causes on this tragic journey.

Trail Conditions:
The Cherokee people were marched hundreds of miles westward, often on foot. Without proper clothing and shelter, they had to deal with dangerously low temperatures. There was a lack of food and clean water, which contributed to the spread of sickness. Many people were weakened by hunger, thirst, and exposure.

Legacy and Repercussions:
The Cherokee Nation and other indigenous communities suffered greatly as a result of the Trail of Tears:

Thousands of Cherokee people perished and their homelands and communities were destroyed as a result of the forced displacement. The loss of contact with their ancestral lands also disrupted cultural and spiritual ties.

2. Impact on Future Generations: The pain and suffering endured by the Cherokee and other indigenous peoples during the Trail of Tears has had a profound and far-reaching influence on generations that followed.

3. Cherokee Resilience: The Cherokee Nation has shown amazing resilience and determination despite the difficulties it has faced. They moved back to what is now Oklahoma and founded prosperous new settlements there.

4. Historical Reflection: The Trail of Tears is a sobering reminder of the wrongs done to Native Americans and the necessity of confronting this traumatic past.

There has been a rising recognition in recent years of the wrongs done to Native American tribes during the Trail of Tears and other times of oppression and forced displacement. Efforts have been made to memorialize the Trail of Tears, keep Cherokee traditions alive, and foster mutual respect and understanding between indigenous communities and the United States.

There is no better symbol of the relocation, dispossession, and misery of Native American peoples than the Trail of Tears. It's a symbol of indigenous peoples' fortitude and shows how far we've come on the path to reconciliation, equality, and justice.

3.3 The effects of economic development and industrialization on the American landscape.

The United States' economic structure, society, and way of life underwent a dramatic upheaval during the time of economic change and industrialization in the late 19th and early 20th centuries. The United States was transformed during this time period into an economic superpower as the industrial revolution, railroad construction, and agricultural revolution all took hold.

The American Age of Industry:
The Industrial Revolution, which had begun in Britain in the late 18th century, reached the United States in the early 19th century. It was marked by the rise of factory production, the widespread adoption of steam power, and the introduction of mechanized labor.

Important Features of Industrialization:

First and foremost, industrialization was driven by the rise of factories and the mass production of goods. The cotton gin and the spinning wheel were just two of the new machinery and technology that completely changed the textile industry.

The creation of canals, steamboats, and railroads, as well as their subsequent extension, improved the transport of both goods and people.

Thirdly, Urbanization occurred when people migrated from the countryside to urban regions in quest of factory jobs brought about by the Industrial Revolution.

Technological Innovations, including the telegraph and the Bessemer steel process, boosted industrialization and the economy even more rapidly.

5. Workforce Shifts: An influx of new workers, many of them immigrants, met the demand of burgeoning businesses.

The introduction of the steel plow and other agricultural innovations, such as crop rotation, boosted output on farms.

Increased Rail Infrastructure:
The expansion of the railroad infrastructure in the United States was a major factor in the country's economic growth during this time period. Rapid railroad expansion linked previously isolated areas and made it easier to transport goods and people. Economic progress and westward expansion were furthered by the 1869 completion of the Transcontinental Railroad, which linked the East and West coasts.

Alterations to Agriculture:
During this time, there were also major shifts in agricultural practice. Steel plows and motorized reapers were two innovations that greatly improved agricultural output. Western farming was revolutionized when new crops like wheat were introduced to the Great Plains. Displacement of Native American tribes and negative effects on the environment were but two of the difficulties brought on by these transformations.

The Power of Corporations:
Standard Oil, Carnegie Steel, and U.S. Steel were just a few of the massive enterprises and trusts that sprang up as a result of the Industrial Revolution. These corporations consolidated power and money by dominating multiple market segments. While they helped the economy expand, worries about monopolies and the resulting concentration of wealth were raised.

Workplace Difficulties:
While industrialization provided economic progress, it also caused issues for workers. Factory work was notorious for its long hours, unsafe conditions, and low pay. Strikes and labor conflicts arose as a result of the emergence of labor organizations advocating for workers' rights.

The Age of Progressivism:
During the Progressive Era of the early 20th century, reform movements attempted to fix the social and economic problems that had arisen as a result of industrialization. Workers' rights, consumer protection, and anti-monopoly laws were all areas of focus during this period of change. To strike a middle ground between economic expansion and social fairness, progressive leaders like Theodore Roosevelt and Woodrow Wilson advocated.

Government Responsibility:
The government was instrumental in steering the economy through transformative times of industrialization. The Sherman Antitrust Act of 1890 intended to restrain monopolistic behaviors, and the Federal Reserve Act of 1913 created a central banking system to regulate the nation's money supply. The Food and Drug Administration and the Interstate Commerce Commission are only two examples of regulatory bodies set up to safeguard consumers.

Global Economic Consequences
The global impact of the United States' economic revolution was significant. The country rose to prominence as a global economic powerhouse. The steel and textile industries in the United States contributed to the country's economic influence abroad by manufacturing commodities for local consumption and export.

Conclusion:
The United States underwent dramatic changes throughout the industrialization and economic upheaval that shaped it into an economic superpower and world leader. Manufacturing, transportation, and business in general all underwent dramatic changes with the industrial revolution. While this age of expansion and invention provided economic success, it also raised serious social, labor, and environmental challenges.

Economic and political issues in the United States are still influenced by the effects of industrialization, the expansion of large corporations, and the difficulties experienced by workers and consumers. This time period is instructive because it highlights America's propensity for invention and advancement and the necessity of addressing the social and economic repercussions of these seismic shifts.

3.4 A Contentious War: Mexico-U.S. Relations

The United States and Mexico both consider the Mexican-American War, which took place between 1846 and 1848, to be a divisive and formative period in their respective histories. The borders, politics, and identities of both countries were profoundly affected by this struggle, which is frequently considered as a continuation of westward expansion and the drive for territorial acquisition.

History and Roots:
It is possible to trace the roots of the Mexican-American War back to a tangled web of historical, political, and territorial disputes:

First, in 1836, what was then a Mexican colony, the Republic of Texas, declared its independence. The Republic of Texas sought annexation by the United States, notwithstanding Mexico's lack of legal recognition of this split.

Second, there were territorial disputes, specifically about the disputed border between Texas and Mexico. The Republic of Texas and the United States of America claimed the Rio Grande delineated their border, while Mexico believed that the Nueces River served as the dividing line.

Third, U.S. Expansionism: The United States attempted to acquire Mexican land in what is now the American Southwest, motivated by the idea of Manifest Destiny and the desire for westward expansion.

4. The Presidency of James K. Polk: Polk, who was elected president in 1845, supported expanding the United States' territory. Tensions rose as a result of his administration's decisions, including as the annexation of Texas and talks to buy California and New Mexico.

5. The Thornton Affair: In 1846, Mexican forces clashed with a United States detachment led by Captain Seth Thornton on the Rio Grande, escalating tensions between the two countries.

The War's Development:
On April 25, 1846, a small group of American soldiers led by General Zachary Taylor clashed with Mexican troops along the Rio Grande, sparking what would become known as the Mexican-American War. Nearly two years were spent fighting a variety of conflicts and campaigns across the globe.

The conflict saw many pivotal events and engagements, including:

1. The Battles of Palo Alto and Resaca de la Palma: These early encounters established U.S. military superiority along the Rio Grande.

Second, the March to California led by General Stephen Kearny saw U.S. soldiers, including the "Army of the West" under Kearny's command, enter California and establish a foothold there.

Third, the United States achieved a major strategic triumph in The Siege of Veracruz by taking control of the Mexican port city of Veracruz.

General Zachary Taylor's men engaged in a major fight in northern Mexico, known as the fight of Buena Vista, which the United States ultimately won.

5. The Capture of Mexico City: In September 1847, under the leadership of General Winfield Scott, U.S. soldiers captured Mexico City.

Guadalupe Hidalgo's Treaty
When the Treaty of Guadalupe Hidalgo was signed on February 2, 1848, the war was officially over. The repercussions of this pact were substantial:

First, by means of the Territorial Cession, Mexico gave the United States a huge chunk of land that now forms the states of California, Nevada, Utah, New Mexico, and Arizona, as well as chunks of the states of Colorado, Wyoming, Kansas, and Oklahoma.

It has been established that the Rio Grande serves as the border between Texas and Mexico.

3. Compensation: The United States agreed to pay Mexico $15 million as part of the deal.

Fourth, the treaty acknowledged the rights of Mexican citizens already residing in the annexed territory.

Implications and Debates:
There is no simple legacy of the Mexican-American War.

First, there is some disagreement over where the conflict actually began; some see it as an aggressive territorial grab motivated by Manifest Destiny.

Human and social impacts 2 The conflict had significant effects on population growth and distribution, especially for Mexicans residing in the annexation territories. Their freedoms, territories, and ways of life were all challenged.

3. Impact on U.S. History: The United States' position as a continental power was bolstered by the war's territorial gains, but growing sectional tensions over the institution of slavery in the newly gained territories exacerbated the situation.

When people in Mexico think back on the conflict, they typically refer to it as the "American Invasion." Despite the fact that it resulted in a decline in territorial control and national independence, this war is nevertheless remembered with great honor.

There is no denying the significance of the Mexican-American War on the development of the United States and Mexico. Expansion, nationalism, and territorial disputes all play a part, and this shows that complexity. The cultural, political, and geographical features of the Southwestern United

States and Mexico have been profoundly affected by this war and its aftermath.

Chapter 4: The Civil War and Reconstruction (1861-1877)

4.1 Causes of the Civil War in the United States

From 1861 to 1865, the United States was embroiled in its bloodiest conflict to date: the American Civil War. The origins of the war, which opposed the Northern states (the Union) against the Southern states (the Confederacy), go back to the founding of the United States. Among the many factors that led to the Civil War were the following:

Slavery, No. 1

The question of slavery was the most contentious and consequential factor that triggered the Civil War. Slavery was institutionalized in the southern states because of their reliance on huge estates and slave labor. However, by the turn of the nineteenth century, the abolitionist movement had gained traction in the Northern states and slavery was effectively outlawed there. A major point of contention was whether or not new areas joining the Union would recognize slavery (popular sovereignty).

2. Disparities in the Economy:

The North and the South had unique economic frameworks. The urban and manufacturing sectors in the North expanded and became more advanced. In contrast, cotton production, which relied primarily on slave labor, was a major economic driver in the South. Regional conflicts were exacerbated by economic inequality.

Third, the Rights of States:

States' rights, or the degree to which individual states may exercise sovereignty apart from the federal government, was a hotly debated topic. Southern states frequently used the concept of state sovereignty to defend slavery and other southern institutions. In contrast, northerners typically favored a more robust central government.

4. Separatism:

When people prioritized their regional identity over national solidarity, this was known as "sectionalism." Culture, economy, and society in the North and South were completely different from one another. This regionalism contributed to an atmosphere of hostility and mistrust between the two areas.

Reason #5: War and Politics

Northern and Southern leaders were increasingly at odds in the political arena. Intense discussions and disagreements arose in Congress over the question of whether or not new territories and states would allow slavery. Attempts to prevent conflict by resolving these issues were made in the Missouri Compromise of 1820, the Compromise of 1850, and the Kansas-Nebraska Act of 1854.

The Abolitionist Movement, Number Six:

Tensions between the North and the South grew as abolitionist sentiment grew in the Northern states. Abolitionist radicals, like John Brown, aimed to overthrow slavery through violent means, further increasing the struggle.

Dred Scott: Number Seven

The Dred Scott ruling in 1857 only made matters worse. The Supreme Court decided that black people in the United States, whether free or enslaved, did not qualify as citizens. Both the moral and legal reasons against further slavery expansion were undermined by this ruling.

John Brown's attack on Harpers Ferry, number eight:

In 1859, John Brown attempted to instigate a slave uprising by raiding the government armory in Harpers Ferry, Virginia. Brown's attempt ultimately failed, and he was apprehended and executed, but it was seen as a symbol of Northern aggression by many in the South and contributed to an already tense situation.

Number Nine: Abraham Lincoln's Election

The election of Abraham Lincoln as the 16th President of the United States in 1860 marked a turning moment. Lincoln, who was against bringing slavery to additional territories, was elected president despite receiving no votes from the South. His victory was seen by many in the South as an attack on their way of life and a possible impetus for secession.

10. Breakaway:

South Carolina was the first of several Southern states to split from the Union after Lincoln was elected. The federal government declared war after these states created the Confederate States of America.

There was a complex interplay of historical, economic, political, and social elements that led to the American Civil War. Slavery was only one of many factors that contributed to the explosive nature of the situation, which eventually erupted into a horrific and destructive war. The Civil War is nevertheless a sobering reminder of the perils of discord and the everlasting value of national harmony.

4.2 Important Civil War Battles and Commanders

From 1861 to 1865, great military men led their respective sides in a succession of pivotal battles during the American Civil War. These battles and leaders were crucial in keeping the Union together and ending slavery, two of the war's most important outcomes. Some of the most important events and figures in the American Civil War include:

1. Battle of Bull Run (First Manassas) :

The battle was significant since it was the first major conflict of the war. The Union's loss highlighted the protracted nature of the war, while the Confederacy's triumph bolstered morale in the South.

Second, the Antietam War:
   Location: Sharpsburg, Maryland; Date: September 17, 1862
   Antietam was the bloodiest single-day combat in American history; it was led by Union Major General George B. McClellan and Confederate General Robert E. Lee. Although strategically indecisive, it provided President Abraham Lincoln the opportunity to issue the Emancipation Proclamation, which declared enslaved citizens in Confederate territory to be free.

Third, the Gettysburg Campaign:
   Location: Gettysburg, Pennsylvania; Dates: July 1-3, 1863
   Importantly, Union forces at Gettysburg halted a Confederate assault of the North, directed by General Robert E. Lee. The Union was led by Major General George G. Meade. It represented the largest and bloodiest combat in the struggle and resulted to a withdrawal of Southern forces, reducing their chances for international intervention.

The Fourth Vicksburg Battle:
   The battle took place between May 18 and July 4, 1863, in Vicksburg, Mississippi. It was led by Union Major General Ulysses S. Grant and Confederate Lt. General John C. Pemberton.

The significance of the Union's successful siege of Vicksburg lies in the fact that it essentially severed the connection between the Western and Eastern Confederacy at the Mississippi River.

Battle of Chattanooga, number five:
The location was Chattanooga, Tennessee, and the date range was November 23-25, 1863.
Major General Ulysses S. Grant led the Union, while General Braxton Bragg led the Confederacy.
Importance: The Union's success at Chattanooga was pivotal because it allowed them to secure control over eastern Tennessee and open supply routes to the beleaguered Army of the Cumberland.

Sixth, the Spotsylvania Court House Battle:
Spotsylvania County, Virginia; the week of May 8-21, 1864
As a part of the Overland Campaign, this fight featured some of the worst trench warfare of the war and was led by Union Lt. Gen. Ulysses S. Grant and Confederate Gen. Robert E. Lee. Although Grant's men did not emerge victorious, their tenacity was on full display.

Sherman's march to the sea, number seven:
Georgia; dates range from November 15th to December 21st, 1864
Union Command: Major General William T. Sherman
Sherman's march from Atlanta to Savannah was crucial because it wiped out so much Southern industry and infrastructure. For the Confederacy, it was a crushing defeat that typified "total war."

The Eighth and Final Battle of Appomattox:
Appomattox Court House, Virginia; Date: April 9, 1865
Importance: The fight and General Lee's capitulation effectively ended the Civil War. - Commanders: Lt. Gen. Ulysses S. Grant (Union) and General Robert E. Lee (Confederacy). It was a pivotal moment in the commencement of the Reconstruction era and the movement toward reunification.

The American Civil War, which tore the country apart and led to the abolition of slavery, turned on these decisive battles and commanders. The war's outcome was affected by the leaders' strategic judgments, their ability to inspire their troops, and their willingness to put themselves in harm's way. It forever altered the course of American history and imparted invaluable lessons about the perils of discord and the power of harmony.

4.3 Emancipation and the abolition of slavery marked a watershed moment in U.S. history.

Lincoln's proclamation of freedom for slaves on January 1, 1863, was a watershed moment in U.S. history. Slaves in Confederate-controlled areas were declared free as a result of this executive order, which paved the way for the eventual abolition of slavery in the United States. Slavery's abolition and eventual emancipation was a long, difficult, and divisive process.

The Proclamation of Emancipation:

The Civil War had already lasted nearly two years when President Lincoln issued the Emancipation Proclamation as a reaction to the conflict. In the words of the Proclamation, "all persons held as slaves" in Confederate territory were to be "then, thenceforward, and forever free." But it didn't instantly end slavery for everyone.

Several crucial components made up the Emancipation Proclamation:

One, it had a limited geographical scope, covering only states that were actively fighting against the Union. This meant that states like Delaware, Maryland, Kentucky, and Missouri, as well as parts of the former Confederate territory that were under Union authority, were exempt.

Second, there is the Military Dimension to consider; the Proclamation was drafted as a military action with the intention of destabilizing the Confederate war effort by liberating slave laborers. Slaves were encouraged to seek safety within Union territory and join the Union Army.

3. Moral Imperative: It expanded the war's reach and represented a moral commitment to abolishing slavery. The fight was framed as one that sought to preserve both the Union and individual liberty.

Four, Precursor to Constitutional Change: The Emancipation Proclamation was a step toward the ratification of the Thirteenth

Amendment to the United States Constitution in December 1865, which finally ended slavery nationwide.

The effects of the Emancipation Proclamation were far-reaching:

When slaves learned of the Proclamation's release, many of them made their way to Union lines in search of freedom. The path to freedom was convoluted and varied greatly from place to region. Some were freed as soon as Union forces arrived, but others remained slaves.

Second, the Dynamics of the War changed as formerly enslaved people won freedom and often joined the Union Army. African-American soldiers were crucial to the Union's success in the war.

Thirdly, Differing Responses were given to the Proclamation. Abolitionists and free Black communities applauded it, but it was met with hatred and resistance in the Confederacy. Despite the Proclamation, slavery remained in some locations until Union forces could put an end to it.

Aftermath:

Slavery in the United States was finally abolished after a chain reaction triggered by the Emancipation Proclamation and the Civil War.

The Thirteenth Amendment to the United States Constitution was ratified in December 1865, thereby ending slavery throughout the country. With the passage of this amendment, the fight to abolish slavery was finally won.

2. Reconstruction Era: During this time period, the South was readmitted to the Union, civil rights laws were passed, and the economic and social repercussions of emancipation were addressed.

3. New Difficulties and Obstacles: During Reconstruction, former slaves faced new difficulties such as discrimination, economic hardship, and the fight for equal rights despite the fact that they were no longer technically

enslaved. The development of civil rights and racial justice movements defined the era.

Legacy:

Important turning points in American history include the proclamation of emancipation and the subsequent abolition of slavery. They stand for the success of democracy over dictatorship, the influence of moral leadership, and the potential for a nation to better itself. Slavery's aftereffects, the fight for civil rights, and the persistence of institutional racism are all factors that continue to define the United States today.

The Emancipation Proclamation is a symbol of the unwavering dedication to the principles of freedom, equality, and justice for all, as well as a call to action to confront structural injustices. It stands as a testimony to the resilience and determination of those who battled for freedom and equality, and as a beacon of hope for the continued pursuit of a more equitable and inclusive society.

4.4 Reconstructing a Fractured Nation during the Era of Reconstruction

The years following the American Civil War, known as the Reconstruction Era, lasted from 1865 to 1877 and were difficult and formative for the United States. Reconstruction efforts, including reuniting the former Confederate states, and dealing with the social, political, and economic fallout of emancipation characterized this time period. Despite its best intentions, the Reconstruction Era was unable to achieve its goal of establishing a more equitable and just society.

There are three stages of rebuilding:

There are three stages of reconstruction:

Reconstruction under the Presidency (1865–1867): 1. Presidential Leadership During this time, President Andrew Johnson, who took office after the assassination of Abraham Lincoln, had a more tolerant stance toward reunifying the South. By ratifying the Thirteenth Amendment (which abolished slavery) and repealing their secession ordinances, Johnson's plan permitted the former Confederate states to re-join the Union. Pre-war Southern political figures reclaimed their positions once the conflict ended.

Impediments and Opposition: Congress and radical Republicans were strongly opposed to Johnson's policy because they felt it did not go far enough to safeguard the rights of former slaves. The Black Codes, discriminatory laws created by Southern governments, attempted to restrict the rights and possibilities of freedpeople.

Second Reconstruction Act of Congress (1867–1869) – Congressional Interference: In response to the failings of Presidential Reconstruction and the discriminatory Black Codes, Radical Republicans in Congress grabbed leadership of the Reconstruction process. In 1867, they approved the Reconstruction Act, which mandated that newly formed state governments in the South grant voting rights to formerly enslaved people and split the region into military districts.

Republican Extreme Successes During this time period, the Fourteenth and Fifteenth Amendments were ratified, respectively guaranteeing citizenship and equal protection under the law and the right to vote for all male citizens regardless of race. Former Confederate officials were also stripped of their voting rights as a result of this.

Third, "Redemption" and the end of Reconstruction (1869-1877) - "Redemption": The "Redemption" process occurred when Northern support for Reconstruction declined and whites in the South regained political authority. This entailed the eventual return of white Democratic authority to the South following the evacuation of federal soldiers.

The Ku Klux Klan and Violent Acts: The violence and discrimination committed by groups like the Ku Klux Klan increased as Reconstruction waned. African Americans and whites who supported Reconstruction were the targets of these attacks.

Compromise reached in 1877: The Compromise of 1877 was an agreement reached after the contentious presidential election of 1876 that saw Republican Rutherford B. Hayes become president in exchange for the withdrawal of federal soldiers from the South. Because of this, segregation and discriminatory legislation known as the Jim Crow era began, effectively ending Reconstruction.

There were both great successes and serious failures throughout the Reconstruction Era.

Achievements:

Freedom and civil rights come in at number one. Slavery was abolished in this century by to the Thirteenth Amendment, citizenship and equal protection were granted in this era thanks to the Fourteenth Amendment, and voting rights were extended to all male citizens in this era according to the Fifteenth Amendment.

2. Economic and Educational Prospects Efforts were made to open schools for freedpeople, and many formerly enslaved people welcomed the opportunity to go to school and further their education.

Thirdly, Black Representation in Politics: Several African Americans were elected to the U.S. Congress and many more held other public offices during Reconstruction.

Shortcomings:

1. Limited Land Reform: The promise of land redistribution to freedpeople did not materialize in a meaningful way, leaving many without economic resources.

(2) "Federal Enforcement Is Canceled" The Compromise of 1877 and the subsequent departure of federal soldiers from the South effectively ended Reconstruction and opened the door to the restoration of white supremacist power in the South.

Violence and Discrimination, 3. The rise of the Ku Klux Klan and the establishment of Jim Crow laws that enforced racial segregation were only two examples of the pervasive violence and discrimination that plagued the time period.

Legacy:

Complexity persists in the wake of the Reconstruction Era. It was a huge step forward for civil rights and racial equality, but it didn't address everything. This time period is significant because it highlights the difficulties of uniting a country that had been torn apart, the ongoing fight for civil rights, and the need to confront the lasting effects of slavery and discrimination. The Reconstruction Era remains pivotal in American history because of the never-ending fight for racial equality and justice.

Chapter 5: The Gilded Age (1877-1900)

5.1 The Impact of Industrialization and Urbanization on American Culture

Industrialization and urbanization radically altered the United States in the late 19th and early 20th century. The Second Industrial Revolution was a time of tremendous development in the United States' industrial and manufacturing sectors, the emergence of cities, and profound shifts in the average American's lifestyle and way of life.

Industrialization:

When a country makes the transition from an agricultural and artisanal economy to one focused on mass manufacturing and machinery, this is known as industrialization. Several significant changes marked the onset of the Second Industrial Revolution:

1. Technological Advances: The Bessemer steel process, the telegraph, and the electric light bulb were just a few of the new technologies that shook up many sectors of the economy. These developments boosted productivity and opened up new avenues for economic expansion.

2. Manufacturing Process: The factory system became the cornerstone of industrial production. Factories allowed for efficient mass production of commodities, leading to the expansion of manufacturing sectors.

Thirdly, "Transportation" and "Railroads:" The increased accessibility of products and people was made possible by the development of the train system. The expansion of trade and the linking of cities across the country were both made possible by railroads.

4. Business Expansion Large firms, such as Standard Oil and U.S. Steel, rose to prominence and cemented their grip over many different

industries throughout this time period. These companies were instrumental in directing economic policy.

Migration and Employment 5. There is now a vast and varied workforce because to the expansion of several sectors. In quest of work in the United States' industries and mines, people from all over the world flooded in.

Urbanization:

The movement of people from rural areas to urban centers is known as urbanization. Changes to the American environment were precipitated by the simultaneous development of urban centers and the industrial economy.

The population of major cities like New York, Chicago, and Philadelphia exploded throughout the last century. The growth of cities as economic, cultural, and creative centers is well documented.

2. Infrastructure and Transportation: Cities expanded their infrastructure to meet the expanding population. Infrastructure projects fell under this category, as did the introduction of public transit and other contemporary conveniences like reliable electricity and clean water.

Housing and Lifestyle Third: Cities quickly became too congested and unfit for human habitation as a result of this inflow of people. Tenements were popular as a kind of housing for the masses, and slums arose as destitute communities of the working class.

Social and Cultural Shifts, No. 4 The spread of cities has brought people from all walks of life closer together. Neighborhoods and communities flourished as a result of the mingling of cultures made possible by this diversity.

Problems and Social Concerns, No. 5 Poverty, criminal activity, and difficulties in delivering public services are just some of the societal problems that emerged in response to urbanization's rapid pace. As a response, social reform initiatives gained momentum as people looked for answers.

Implications for the Economy and Society:

Wide-ranging and intricate, the effects of industrialization and urbanization include:

Economic expansion The United States economy expanded substantially during this time. Industries expanded, and the nation's wealth increased.

Second, Improved Living Standards: As a result of industrialization, many Americans were able to raise their quality of living and get access to previously unavailable consumer items.

The Labor Movement 3. The labor movement was spurred by the increasing number of factories and the migration of workers to urban areas. Workers formed unions to bargain for higher pay, safer working conditions, and other worker protections.

Innovations in Technology The invention of the telephone, the vehicle, and the airplane were just a few of the many advances made possible by the Second Industrial Revolution.

Disparities in social status: The growth of industry and cities further exacerbated existing socioeconomic divisions. Some did well, but others were exploited and starved to death. To combat these inequalities, social reform movements developed.

Changes in Culture, No. 6 As a result of the societal transformations, new art, literature, and entertainment emerged to depict city life.

Legacy:

The current United States may trace its origins back to the era of industrialization and urbanization. It reshaped the country's economy, infrastructure, and social fabric, paving the way for the expansion and progress that characterized the 20th century. Economic expansion, urban development, and social progress are still referenced today because of the opportunities and challenges that arose during this time.

5.2 The Fight for Workers' Rights, the History of Labor Movements

The United States' labor laws, working conditions, and societal and economic landscape could not be what they are today without the contributions of labor movements. Beginning in the late 19th and early 20th centuries, these movements played a significant role in promoting workers' rights, equal pay, and safer workplaces. There have been many successes and failures throughout their history, but they have never stopped trying to better the lives of American workers.

Labor Movements' Emergence:

Labor movements in the United States began to gain strength throughout the late 19th century as industrialization and urbanization altered the nation's economic landscape. Wage labor became more prevalent as factories and other industrial businesses expanded rapidly. Workers in these fields generally faced long hours, low pay, dangerous conditions, and a lack of job security. The following are examples of important elements that contributed to the rise of labor movements:

One major issue was the exploitation of factory and mine workers, both men and women and children. They worked long hours with dangerous equipment and lived in squalor.

Lackluster Pay: Many workers were paid wages that were so low that they couldn't even satisfy their most fundamental needs. The need for higher pay was fueled in part by the recent economic downturn.

3. Lack of work Security: Workers often had minimal work security, with employers allowed to hire and fire at will. Workers were worried about their lack of job security and stability.

4. Disparities in Socioeconomic Status: The necessity for fair treatment and labor reform was highlighted by the wide disparity in income between industrialists and workers.

Important Struggles and Wins for Labor:

There were a number of different labor movements happening at the same time, all with their own aims and methods. The following are examples of labor movements that achieved notable results:

The Labor Knights (1) The Knights of Labor, one of the earliest nationwide labor unions, was established in 1869. It aimed to promote an eight-hour workday, safer working conditions, and shorter workweeks. When it came to fighting for workers' rights and improving the labor system, the Knights of Labor were indispensable.

Second, The American Federation of Labor (AFL): Established in 1886, the AFL was a federation of labor unions that largely focused on skilled workers. The American Federation of Labor, led by people like Samuel Gompers, advocated for things like improved working conditions, greater salaries, and the right to bargain collectively.

3. The International Workers' (IWW) Union: The International Workers of the World, or Wobblies, were a radical labor organization founded in 1905. They were vocal advocates of industrial unionism, which sought to bring together workers of all backgrounds and specializations.

The Triangle Shirtwaist Factory Fire, Number Four: A catalyst for labor reform, the Triangle Shirtwaist Factory fire in 1911 claimed the lives of 146 workers because of dangerous working conditions. As a result, people began to realize how important it was to implement more stringent safety measures in the workplace.

In 1935, President Franklin D. Roosevelt signed into law the National Labor Relations Act (NLRA), which guaranteed workers the freedom to join unions and negotiate collectively in an effort to improve their living standards during the Great Depression.

The Civil Rights Movement, Number Six: The labor movement of the 1950s and 1960s was profoundly affected by the Civil Rights Movement.

Anti-discrimination rules and legislation were enacted after the fight for civil rights spread to the workplace.

Persistent Obstacles and Difficulties:

Workers' rights, fair salaries, and better working conditions have improved thanks to labor movements, but many problems and fights remain.

First, the persistent problem of income disparity in the United States. While labor movements have helped many people, wealth and income gaps still exist.

Globalization, secondly: Challenges to job stability and workers' rights have arisen as a result of globalization of labor markets due to greater competition and outsourcing.

Thirdly, Technological Development and Automation: Automation and other technological advancements have altered the nature of work, which could have far-reaching effects on the job market and workers' stability.

The Gig Economy 4. Worker classification, benefits, and rights have all been complicated by the advent of the gig economy.

"Minimum Wage" 5. The fight to raise the federal minimum wage to a level where workers can make a decent living income continues.

Collective bargaining and the right to fair representation in the workplace are still issues that labor organizations and workers are fighting for.

Conclusion:

Labor movements in the United States have been essential in pushing for workers' rights and labor reform, resulting to considerable changes in workplace conditions and job security. Despite ongoing difficulties, the legacies of these campaigns highlight the significance of maintaining the fight for all American workers to receive fair treatment, fair wages, and better working conditions. An integral part of America's dedication to economic and social fairness is the fight for workers' rights.

5.3 Technological Progress: Molding the Future

Changes in people's lifestyles, occupations, and social interactions have been spurred by technological progress, which has been a major factor in the development of human society. In the United States, as in much of the globe, the 19th and 20th centuries witnessed a series of transformational breakthroughs that reshaped the terrain of daily living, communication, transportation, industry, and conflict. These developments not only benefited many people, but they also presented new opportunities and problems that are still shaping the globe today.

The birth of instantaneous communication with the invention of the telegraph.

The telegraph was a revolutionary invention that greatly impacted human communication in the 19th century. In 1837, Samuel Morse and his colleagues established the first telegraph connection and created the Morse code. As early as 1844, the first telegraph message was sent between the nation's capital and Baltimore. This innovation completely changed the way that people could communicate over great distances. The telegraph was essential in the dissemination of information, laying the groundwork for the development of the modern communications sector.

The Incandescent Light Bulb

Thomas Edison's discovery of the electric light bulb in 1879 was another significant advance in technology. Light from Edison's invention transformed daily life by allowing people to work late into the night, changing the course of history. Because of the electric light bulb, industries could now function around the clock, greatly increasing industrial output.

A Word About That Car:

In the early 20th century, the invention of the vehicle radically altered the transportation landscape. In 1908, Henry Ford revolutionized the automobile industry by mass producing the Model T using an assembly line. The development of the automobile industry is just one example of how this innovation has altered the face of the United States. The advent of the personal automobile and its convenient means of transportation radically altered city layouts and fostered the growth of exurban areas and a culture centered on the automobile that has persisted to the present day.

The Aeroplane:

In Kitty Hawk, North Carolina, in 1903, the Wright brothers Orville and Wilbur made the first powered, controlled, and sustained flight. Their discovery paved the way for future developments in aviation, including passenger planes, fighter planes, and satellite communication. By decreasing travel times and costs, air travel has boosted worldwide commerce, tourism, and cultural understanding.

The World Wide Web

The internet, a technology that would radically alter the way people interact and share knowledge, emerged in the second part of the twentieth century. The Internet is a worldwide system that has grown from its roots in the 1960s to link individuals, businesses, and technological gadgets all over the world. It has changed how we learn, work, talk to one other, and socialize. The internet has had a profound impact on the development of the information age.

Improvements and Threats:

While technology progress has unquestionably enhanced many facets of modern living, it has also introduced novel difficulties.

The Digital Divide There is a digital divide since not everyone has the same options when it comes to online learning, employment, and democracy.

Concerns About Privacy Concerns regarding privacy and data security have surfaced alongside the expansion of the internet and digital technology. Companies and governments' gathering and use of personal data has sparked heated discussion and calls for stricter regulation.

Thirdly, "Automation and Job Loss:" Industries and labor marketplaces are changing as a result of automation and AI. While these innovations improve productivity, they also pose the risk of eliminating some jobs and causing other changes in the demand for human labor.

4. Impact on the Environment: Electronic waste, energy usage, and carbon emissions from data centers are only a few examples of the environmental effects of technology's widespread use. Sustainable technology development and appropriate usage are continuous problems.

5. Threats to Cybersecurity The capacity of cybercriminals to exploit security holes in digital systems grows in tandem with the development of new technologies. The necessity for robust cybersecurity measures to secure data and key infrastructure is paramount.

Conclusion:

Our manner of life, our methods of production, and our social interactions have all been revolutionized by technological innovation. These technological advances, beginning with the telegraph and continuing with the internet, have had far-reaching effects on all facets of modern life. The prospects for creativity, economic progress, and the betterment of human existence that have resulted from technological advances have been enormous, but they have also brought new obstacles. The development of technology is important to the story of human evolution and progress.

5.4 American Identity as a Mosaic, Shaped by Immigration and Cultural Shifts

Since its inception, immigration has been a driving force in defining the cultural environment of the United States. Immigrants from all over the world have woven their own cultural patterns into the fabric of America, shaping its language, cuisine, art, religion, and social traditions. The United States is a dynamic nation, and its cultural diversity is in large part due to the ebb and flow of immigration, which has brought both possibilities and challenges.

Migration Trends Through Time:

Multiple waves of immigration have shaped American culture, and each has left its own distinctive mark on the country:

The Colonial Period (1): The English, Dutch, Spanish, and French colonists who came to North America first established the country's infrastructure. They spread their own customs, languages, and religions to other areas, so shaping local history and culture.

There was a large influx of immigrants in the 19th century, particularly of Irish, German, and Chinese origin. Germans sought greater economic possibilities, while Irish fled the Great Famine in Ireland. The California Gold Rush drew Chinese immigrants, some of whom eventually helped build the Transcontinental Railroad.

Time Period 3: (Late 19th/Early 20th) During this time, millions of people—most notably Italians, Poles, and Jews—arrived in the United States, marking the beginning of the so-called "Great Wave" of immigration. Urban culture flourished as a result of the integration of these previously marginalized communities into mainstream American life.

4. The Migration of African-Americans: Millions of African Americans left the Jim Crow South for the industrial cities of the North during the early

20th century, a period known as the Great Migration. The arts, especially music, literature, and civil rights advocacy, were deeply influenced by this internal migration.

5. Immigration from Asia: Significant numbers of people from Asia, particularly China, Japan, the Philippines, and South Asia, migrated to other parts of the world in the twentieth century. Culture of the United States has been enriched by the contributions of many different groups.

Modern Immigration: Recent decades have seen a sustained impact on American culture from people who came to the country from Latin America, the Caribbean, Africa, the Middle East, and Asia. They have contributed to the richness of American culture by shaping its cuisine, music, and language.

Contributions to Culture and Challenges to Culture:

Immigration has benefited American culture and presented new challenges to it.

The influence of immigrants on American food is obvious. American diners can't get enough of pasta, tacos, stir-fry, and shawarma from Italy, Mexico, China, and the Middle East.

Tongue: 2. The United States' linguistic variety is a reflection of the many immigrant groups that have established here. The rise of bilingualism and multilingualism has enriched American discourse with new perspectives and perspectives.

American popular culture has been profoundly impacted by the contributions of immigrant populations. Examples of music and movies that have benefited greatly from the contributions of minorities include jazz and hip-hop, both of which have their origins in African American culture.

Religion, number four Diverse religious customs and observances were brought to the United States by immigrant populations. There is a rich variety of religions present in this area, including Buddhism, Islam, Hinduism, and numerous branches of Christianity.

5. Difficulties: Cultural assimilation concerns, language problems, and discussions of how to strike a balance between cultural preservation and integration are all issues that have arisen as a result of immigration.

Cultural mosaic vs. melting pot:

The idea of the "melting pot," which depicts many cultural groups merging together to generate a single united culture, has long been used to describe American civilization. However, the idea of a "cultural mosaic" has become increasingly popular, with its focus on the acceptance and appreciation of cultural differences without compromising on any of them. The United States is becoming more widely recognized as a nation where people of different cultural backgrounds may successfully coexist.

Conclusion:

Immigration has been a driving force in developing the unique American culture that we know today. While immigration has increased cultural diversity in the United States, it has also raised concerns about assimilation and cultural loss. The United States of America is a dynamic and diverse nation because of the many cultures that cohabit here. As the United States continues its story of expansion, change, and renewal, immigration and the resulting cultural shifts remain vital components of the national narrative.

Chapter 6: Progressive Era and World War I (1900-1920)

6.1 The Progressive Era: A Watershed Moment in U.S. History

A major turning point in American history occurred during the Progressive Era, which lasted from the late 19th century to the early 20th century. In response to the problems caused by industrialization, urbanization, and social inequality, the United States saw a wave of social and political reform during this time. Political corruption, labor exploitation, women's suffrage, and economic control were only some of the problems that progressive reforms attempted to solve.

Historical Context for the Progressive Era:

The United States experienced unprecedented economic expansion and industrialization throughout the latter half of the nineteenth century. These changes brought about greater affluence, but they also brought about a host of social and economic problems. There have been calls for change because of problems such rapid urbanization, income disparity, and labor exploitation.

Important Changes Made During the Progressive Era:

Numerous changes, affecting several facets of American life, were implemented during the Progressive Era. Among the most significant changes were:

1. Reforms to the Political System - Senate Elections by Popular Vote The 17th Amendment to the Constitution (1913) prohibited state legislatures from appointing senators and instead required that senators be elected directly by the people. The goal of this change was to lessen graft in government.
   Recall, Referendum, and Initiative: Various states utilized these democratic instruments, allowing individuals to propose laws (initiative),

vote on new laws (referendum), and remove elected persons from office (recall).

Second, Labor Laws and Regulations: Labor Reforms, such as Limiting Working Hours, Improving Workplace Safety, and Establishing a Minimum Wage, were strongly supported by progressive leaders.
 - Unionization of the Workforce: Unions defending workers' rights, such as the American Federation of Labor (AFL) and the Industrial Workers of the World (IWW), gained traction during this time period.

Thirdly, the Suffrage for Women - The progressive era was a pivotal time for the women's suffrage movement. It was a huge stride forward for women's rights when the 19th Amendment was ratified in 1920 and finally gave them the vote.

The purpose of consumer protection legislation is to prevent people from being harmed by substandard or fraudulent goods. There were two laws passed in 1906 with the same goal in mind—the Pure Food and Drug Act and the Meat Inspection Act.

Fifth, Economic Regulation and Antitrust - During the Progressive Era, antitrust laws were enacted to limit the influence of multinational firms and prohibit monopolistic behavior. Important laws in this area include the Sherman Antitrust Act (1890) and the Clayton Antitrust Act (1914).

6. Environmental Conservation: - The conservation movement, led by personalities like President Theodore Roosevelt, focused on protecting natural resources and building national parks and monuments. In 1916, the National Park Service was established to manage the parks.

Problems and Disagreements:

There was resistance to progressive changes from influential economic groups and political conservatives. Some critics of progressive reforms said that they threatened personal freedoms and the free market because of the government's growing role in society.

Reforms left behind by progressivism:

Progressive changes have left a profound and long-lasting legacy. Modern welfare states and regulatory frameworks owe a great deal to the era's radical reworking of the government's role in the economy. Some important features of this legacy are:

One, Greater Government Regulation: Progressive reforms laid the groundwork for government intervention in the economy, consumer protection, worker rights, and environmental conservation.

2. Empowerment of Citizens: Progressive reforms attempted to offer citizens a more direct involvement in crafting government policies and addressing concerns at the state and national levels through initiatives, referendums, recalls, and the direct election of senators.

3. Advancement of Civil Rights: The women's suffrage campaign was a critical step in the ongoing struggle for civil rights and gender equality in the United States.

The environmental conservation movement laid the groundwork for the careful curation of the nation's natural heritage and the prudent management of its natural resources, which brings us to our fourth point: Protection of Natural Resources.

The Progressive Era reflects a time when Americans tackled the issues of a rapidly changing society and took action to meet them. These changes were a turning point in American history, and their effects may still be felt today in the way people think about and interact with their government.

6.2 A History of Women's Fight for Voting Rights and Equality

The fight for women's suffrage in the United States was a long and difficult one. Women and their supporters fought for decades to win the vote, and in 1920, after much effort, the 19th Amendment was ratified. In addition to granting women the right to vote, this historic victory also established a firm groundwork for future improvements in women's rights.

Women's rights activists from the beginning:

Early 19th-century activists like Susan B. Anthony and Elizabeth Cady Stanton laid the groundwork for the modern women's suffrage movement. The Seneca Falls Convention, which these women and others convened in 1848, is often regarded as the beginning of the modern women's rights movement. The Declaration of Sentiments, written at the convention, similarly echoed the wording of the Declaration of Independence in calling for women's equality and the ability to vote.

In the decades that followed, the suffrage campaign gained even more support. There was tremendous pushback against women's rights campaigners from people who thought their involvement in politics was pointless or even harmful. Despite these obstacles, suffragists continued working to gain support for their cause through a variety of means.

Civil Disobedience and Activism: Suffragists participated in picketing, hunger strikes, and public protests as forms of civil disobedience. These strategies were effective in getting the word out and gaining momentum for the suffrage cause.

Education and Advocacy:
Women's rights activists who advocated for the vote made numerous public appearances across the country to spread their message. To reach more people, they distributed booklets and newsletters.

Success on the State Level:
Many states had already granted women the vote before the 19th Amendment was passed, demonstrating the movement's success at the state level. In 1869, Wyoming made history by granting women the right to vote.

The Nineteenth Amendment

Women's suffrage in the United States reached a major milestone with the passage of the 19th Amendment to the Constitution. The amendment was adopted on August 18, 1920, following its passage by Congress on June 4, 1919. It read, "The right of citizens of the United States to vote shall not be denied or abridged by the United States or by any State on account of sex."

Influence and Aftermath:

The passage of the 19th Amendment was a significant step forward in the campaign for gender equality in the United States. Women won the right to vote and their participation in politics became a cornerstone of the American political system.

First and foremost, women's suffrage allowed for a greater number of women to take part in politics and run for office. Women have held a wide variety of political positions over the years, from mayor to governor to congresswoman to presidential nominee.

Second, the fight for women's suffrage cleared the way for subsequent victories for women's rights, such as equal pay for equal work and the ability to choose whether or not to have children. It was helpful in questioning stereotypical gender roles and norms.

Three levels of intersectionality: Although white women reaped the most direct benefits from the suffrage campaign, the groundwork was created for later activism on behalf of women of color and other disenfranchised groups. Many women fought for equal rights for all people, including Sojourner Truth, Ida B. Wells, and others.

4. Persistent Challenges: While substantial progress has been made, the fight for gender equality continues. In the continuous discussion about women's rights, concerns like equal pay, ending violence against women, and ensuring universal healthcare access all remain central.

Conclusion:

Many women and their male allies worked tirelessly to bring about a sea change in American history through the women's suffrage movement. Women's suffrage and the continued fight for equal rights and social justice were given a major boost with the enactment of the 19th Amendment. Contemporary campaigns for gender equality and the advancement of women's rights draw inspiration and insight from the suffrage movement's legacy.

6.3 The Great War: A Global Conflict That Forged the Twentieth Century.

The First World War, or the Great War, began in 1914 and lasted until 1918 on every continent. Many of the world's major powers were involved in this conflict, which had far-reaching effects on the century's politics, economy, and culture. International relations and global dynamics are still being molded by its aftereffects.

The Root Causes of WWI

The initiation of World War I was influenced by a number of interconnected variables. Militarism, alliances, imperialism, and nationalism were among these. When Archduke Franz Ferdinand, ruler of Austria-Hungary, was killed in Sarajevo in 1914, it sparked World War I. A series of alliances and war declarations among the main European nations followed Austria-Hungary's declaration of war on Serbia.

Conflict between the Central Powers and the Allies:

The primary players in the fight formed two separate coalitions. Germany, Austria-Hungary, the Ottoman Empire, and Bulgaria made up what were known as the Central Powers. France, the United Kingdom, Russia, and the United States joined the Entente Powers, or the Allies.

The Stalemate and Trench Warfare:

The Western Front was notorious for its bloody trench fighting, in which men faced constant peril in appalling conditions. Millions of men died during this stage of the war, which was characterized by stalemates and limited territorial advances. Machine guns, chemical weapons, and tanks all contributed to an already difficult and bloody conflict.

With America's entry into the conflict:

At first, the United States took a stand of neutrality. However, as the war progressed, numerous circumstances prompted the United States to enter the war on the side of the Allies in April 1917. These included Germany's unrestricted submarine warfare and the Zimmermann Telegram, which exposed Germany's plan to combine with Mexico against the U.S.

As the War Comes to a Close:

In 1918, the Central Powers collapsed as a result of the Allies' successful offensives and the internal struggle and economic troubles within the Central Powers. A ceasefire was declared after the signing of an armistice on November 11, 1918. The war was formally ended with the signing of the Treaty of Versailles in 1919, which rearranged European borders and imposed severe punishments on Germany.

Effects of World War I:

First, the human cost of World War I was astronomical. About 10 million soldiers were killed and many more were injured during the war. It is estimated that between 6 and 13 million civilians died as a direct result of the war.

Political Shifts 2. Important political shifts occurred as a result of the war, including the fall of powerful empires like the Austro-Hungarian, Ottoman, and Russian ones. Maps of Europe and the Middle East were redrawn and national borders were rearranged as a result of the Treaty of Versailles.

3) Financial Repercussions There were significant economic repercussions from the war. Many countries' economies collapsed, and inflation and debt skyrocketed as a result. It also prepared the foundation for the economic issues of the interwar period.

4. Impact on Culture: The conflict had a major effect on popular culture. Many musicians and writers reflected on the atrocities and disillusionment of the war, and their work was reflected in popular

culture. Gertrude Stein coined the term "Lost Generation" to represent the generation of young people who were devastated by World War II.

5. League of Nations: The League of Nations was formed after World War I as a means of fostering international cooperation and averting further war. The League's good intentions were not enough to stop the start of World War II, however.

Causes that led up to WWII(6) World conflict II's preconditions were helped along by the economic troubles that followed the conflict and the unresolved concerns and punishing nature of the Treaty of Versailles.

Number Seven: The Redefinition of the Middle East: The collapse of the Ottoman Empire led to the redrawing of borders in the Middle East, forming modern nation-states in the region. It has far-reaching effects on international politics.

Conclusion:

The First World War was the defining event of the twentieth century. It changed the course of history by laying the groundwork for future wars and cultural shifts. The lessons of the conflict, including the importance of international cooperation through bodies like the United Nations, are still applicable today. The devastating effects of World War I emphasize the need for peaceful means of conflict resolution and the maintenance of international harmony.

6.4 Fear, suspicion, and the remaking of American society during the Red Scare

Fear and suspicion of communism and other radical political ideas surged throughout the United States at the turn of the twentieth century, a time known as the Red Scare. Significantly influencing the national response to social and political change throughout this tumultuous century, it had far-reaching effects on American culture, politics, and civil liberties.

The Initial Fear of Communism (1919–1921)

Several events, including the 1917 Russian Revolution that installed a communist government in Russia, set off the First Red Scare. Concerns about radicalism were driven by the fear of communist ideology spreading to the United States as well as labor strikes and civil upheaval in the years following World War I. The characteristics of the Red Scare were:

"1. "Palmer Raids" A series of raids and arrests were led by Attorney General A. Mitchell Palmer to pick up suspected radicals and anarchists. Many thousands of people were detained and deported.

Anti-immigrant sentiment spiked during the Red Scare, prompting the establishment of quotas for different nationalities in the Immigration Act of 1924.

Restricting Individual Rights (3) During this time, civil rights such as the right to free speech and assembly were restricted. The government utilized the Espionage Act of 1917 and the Sedition Act of 1918 to suppress critics and put them behind bars.

The Period of the Second Red Scare, 1947–1957

Fears of communist infiltration into American society and government gave rise to the Second Red Scare, often known as McCarthyism, in the decades following World War II. Increased anti-communist hysteria was largely due to Senator Joseph McCarthy's efforts. Characteristics of the Second Red Scare included:

1. The Black List in Hollywood: The impact of the Second Red Scare on the entertainment business was significant. Many actors, directors, and writers were blacklisted when the House Un-American Activities Committee (HUAC) looked into the communist influence in Hollywood.

Second, the Lavender Panic There was a "Lavender Scare" directed toward the LGBTQ community during the Second Red Scare, in addition to the anti-communist fury. Many public servants lost their jobs because of their assumed sexual orientation.

HUA hearings, 3. Hearings held by the HUAC were widely publicized and used to interrogate suspects on their supposed communist ties. Some witnesses, including the "Hollywood Ten," were convicted for contempt of Congress for refusing to participate.

Impact and Alterations in Social Life:

Rather than being isolated incidents of political panic, the Red Scares had far-reaching and long-lasting consequences for American culture and government.

Terrorism and bigotry Fear and bigotry flourished as a result of the Red Scares. Many citizens hid their political leanings and affiliations out of fear of being wrongly charged.

The repression of civil liberties, especially the freedoms of expression and assembly, during both Red Scares prompted serious reflection on the trade-offs between national security and individual liberty.

The Use of Anti-Communism in Politics, 3. Political goals were advanced through the employment of anti-communism, and McCarthyism in particular came to be associated with baseless allegations and personal destruction.

4. Impact on Foreign Policy: The Red Scares influenced U.S. foreign policy, particularly in its position against the Soviet Union during the Cold War. Concern over the spread of communism abroad prompted the implementation of containment policies and the backing of anti-communist governments around the world.

5 - Social Activism Social activism received a boost from the Red Scares. Many groups and people fought back against McCarthyism and for equality and freedom of expression. Conflicts against McCarthyism influenced the development of contemporary civil rights and liberties movements.

Conclusion:

Fear, distrust, and the stifling of civil liberties characterized the United States during the Red Scares. They had a long-lasting effect on politics, culture, and the treatment of people and groups seen as challenges to the status quo in the United States. Increased anti-communism during times of social and political turmoil highlights the precarious balance that must be maintained between national security and individual liberties.

Chapter 7: The Roaring Twenties and the Great Depression (1920-1940)

7.1 A Cultural Revolution that Set the World on Fire: Jazz Era America

The Jazz Age, often known as the Roaring Twenties, was an exciting and revolutionary time in American history, when many established customs and values were discarded and new ones established. The Jazz Age, with its emphasis on defiance, hedonism, and social revolution, left a lasting effect on American society that is being felt today.

World War I left the world unsettled and generated a need for emancipation and celebration, both of which helped pave the way for the emergence of the Jazz Age. The decade of the 1920s was marked by rising wealth and revolutionary changes in technology, popular culture, and the arts.

Jazz and Music's Radical New Era:

Jazz, a musical genre with its origins in African and African-American cultures, was a driving force during the Jazz Age. It was a symbol of individuality, innovation, and defiance. Jazz musicians like Louis Armstrong, Duke Ellington, and Bessie Smith came to symbolize an entire age, and their music expressed the hopes and aspirations of its listeners. Jazz was more than a passing fad; it was a cultural revolution that broke down barriers of color and class.

Alterations in Society and the Flapper Scene:

The position of women in society shifted dramatically throughout the Jazz Age. The "flapper" became a cultural icon that stood for the newfound confidence and self-determination of young women. Flappers' bobbed hair, short skirts, and free-thinking attitudes were a direct challenge to the norms of the day. They were against the status quo because they wanted to express themselves freely.

Speakeasies and the Prohibition Era:

One of the most memorable characteristics of the Jazz Age was Prohibition, the statewide ban on the sale and consumption of alcohol. While the law was meant to encourage moderation, it instead spawned a vibrant underground culture of speakeasies, or hidden bars. Speakeasies were places where people congregated and socialized, and they played a vital role in encouraging defiance against authorities.

Explosion in Literature and the Arts:

The 1920s were a time of great creative ferment in the arts and literature. Perhaps the most well-known book from the era is "The Great Gatsby" by F. Scott Fitzgerald, which perfectly captures the decadence and disillusionment of its day. Writers and poets like Ernest Hemingway and Langston Hughes helped weave together the vibrant literary fabric of the time. African American literary, musical, and artistic expression flourished throughout the Jazz Age with the development of the Harlem Renaissance.

Advances in Technology:

The widespread availability of the automobile and the radio, both products of technological progress, helped bring people together. The automobile provided for greater mobility and freedom, enabling a more integrated society. The radio's versatility in broadcasting news, music, and entertainment aided in the proliferation of pop culture and the popularity of jazz.

The Business Cycle:

There was a period of economic growth in the 1920s, but it did not benefit everyone. Despite widespread prosperity and increased free time, wide socioeconomic gaps remained. The Great Depression, which began with the Wall Street Crash of 1929, put an end to the Jazz Age.

Influence and Lasting Impact:

American culture and society are still feeling the effects of the Jazz Age today. Resistance to authority, openness to new ideas, and the need to express oneself have all left indelible marks. The cultural transformations of the Jazz Age paved the way for later social and political movements including the civil rights movement, the feminist movement, and LGBTQ+ activism, and jazz music continues to be an iconic American art form.

Conclusion:

The Jazz Age was a moment of social, cultural, and artistic change in the United States. Jazz music blasted out, the flapper era took off, and people rebelled against the status quo. The Jazz Age forever altered American culture by questioning accepted conventions, praising uniqueness, and welcoming change. It captured the lively energy of the Roaring Twenties, a time of radical change and lasting impact.

7.2 A Catastrophic Prelude to the Great Depression: The 1929 Stock Market Crash

One of the most infamous days in American economic history was Black Tuesday, when the stock market crashed in 1929. It was a watershed moment that ushered in the Great Depression, an era of devastation in both economic and social conditions. The crash had far-reaching effects, fundamentally altering government policy, financial regulation, and social welfare in the wake of its effects on the economy.

The United States enjoyed a prosperous era known as the Roaring Twenties in the years before the Great Depression. A combination of irrational exuberance and speculative buying drove up stock prices. Excessive borrowing and speculative trading occurred because many people falsely assumed the stock market was immune to major falls.

The Triggering Incidents:

The stock market crashed on October 29, 1929, wiping out billions of dollars in value overnight. Several things came together to cause the precipitous decline:

First, Overvalued Stocks: Many companies were trading at extremely high prices compared to their actual earnings, pushing stock prices to unsustainable levels.

Second, a speculative bubble formed when investors became overconfident that stock prices would continue to grow indefinitely and borrowed significantly to buy stocks.

3. Panic Buying Panic ensued when stock prices fell, triggering a widespread selling event. Investors and traders hurriedly sold their assets, speeding up the fall.

Financial Panic of 2008: The crash had a cascading effect on the banking system, as many banks had invested substantially in equities. The subsequent bank runs and credit shortages triggered a serious economic crisis.

Implications for the Economy:

There were serious and long-lasting economic repercussions from the 1929 stock market crash.

Great Depression (1): The crash heralded the start of the Great Depression, a time of great economic misery that saw widespread joblessness, company collapses, and extreme poverty.

Millions of Americans have lost their jobs, and the unemployment rate has risen sharply as a result. People had a hard time making ends meet, and as a result, spending fell dramatically across the country.

3. Failed Businesses Large and small companies alike collapsed. A crisis hit rural America as industrial productivity dropped and the agriculture sector encountered its own set of difficulties.

Bank Runs 4. Many banks failed as a result of the financial crisis, wiping out the life savings of countless Americans. There was a crisis of confidence and banks was under extreme stress.

The government took three major actions in response to the economic disaster caused by the crash:

The New Deal was a series of initiatives created by President Franklin D. Roosevelt in the 1930s to aid in the country's recovery and reform. Social Security, UI, and the Civilian Conservation Corps all helped the unemployed find work at this time.

The Securities and Exchange Commission (SEC): The Securities and Exchange Commission (SEC) was set up to ensure the integrity of the stock market by regulating the securities business and safeguarding investors against scams.

Banking Reforms (3) The Banking Act of 1933, also known as the Glass-Steagall Act, established a firewall between commercial and investment banking to protect depositors' money from speculative risk.

The Federal Deposit Insurance Corporation was set up to safeguard people's bank deposits.

Implications and Lessons:

The Great Depression that followed the Stock Market Crash of 1929 had long-lasting effects on American culture and politics. It highlighted the need for fiscal and monetary policy responsibility, social safety nets, and financial regulation. Crashing markets are a sobering reminder of the dangers of speculative excess and the possibility of economic collapse when they become untethered from underlying economic conditions.

Conclusion:

When the stock market crashed in 1929, it set off a decade of economic suffering and social unrest known as the Great Depression. It had far-reaching effects, including extensive government intervention and regulation of the financial industry, which in turn changed the national economy. The crash and the accompanying Great Depression are essential chapters in American economic history, delivering critical lessons on the necessity of financial stability, responsible government, and the protection of individuals and their savings.

7.3 The New Deal and FDR: A Game-Changing Approach to the Great Depression.

The New Deal enacted by Franklin D. Roosevelt (FDR) was a watershed point in American history. The Great Depression ushered in a new age of government intervention and social safety nets under FDR's leadership and the New Deal's array of initiatives, which aimed to offer relief, recovery, and change.

The Great Depression, for context.

After the stock market crash of 1929, the United States entered a period of extraordinary economic distress known as the Great Depression. There was widespread poverty and joblessness in the United States, impacting millions of people. The nation's economy and social fabric were collapsing, and people were losing hope.

The First New Deal Under FDR's Direction:

In 1932, when Franklin D. Roosevelt became president, the United States was facing some of its darkest days. He moved quickly to solve the economic catastrophe, kicking off the program that would be known as the First New Deal.

Important Aspects of the Original New Deal:

One example of FDR's banking reforms was his declaration of a banking holiday, during which banks were closed briefly to avoid additional panic. The purpose of the Emergency Banking Act was to increase trust in financial institutions.

Programs of Aid Unemployed young men could find work with the Civilian Conservation Corps (CCC). Large-scale public works projects were funded by the Public Works Administration (PWA), while millions of Americans found work through the Civil Works Administration (CWA).

Thirdly, Social Security: The Social Security Act of 1935 laid the groundwork for the present social safety net by creating a system of retirement benefits and unemployment insurance.

Fourth, Securities Legislation: To oversee the securities market and safeguard investors, Congress in 1934 enacted the Securities Exchange Act, which established the Securities and Exchange Commission (SEC).

agricultural Income Stabilization is the goal of the Agricultural Adjustment Act (AAA), which aimed to do so by limiting agricultural output and increasing crop prices.

Comments on the New Deal II:

The First New Deal achieved a great deal, but it was not without its detractors. Both liberal and conservative critics questioned the usefulness of these initiatives. In response, FDR instituted a more active role for the government in the economy during the Second New Deal.

Important Elements of the New Deal's Second Round

First, the WPA (Works Progress Administration): Construction of roads, bridges, and government buildings were just some of the millions of WPA jobs created. It helped creative types like authors, too.

National Labor Relations Act, Section 301 Workers' ability to form unions and engage in collective bargaining with their employers was protected by the Wagner Act of 1935.

Thirdly, the Second New Deal boosted the reach of Social Security and the number of people who receive benefits.

The Rural Energy for America Program (REA): Millions of Americans' standard of living was raised thanks to the REA's efforts to bring power to rural areas.

The New Deal's Lasting Impact

The New Deal had far-reaching and long-lasting effects on the United States:

Initial "Social Safety Nets" Social Security and unemployment insurance are only two examples of how the New Deal paved the way for today's welfare state in the United States.

Regulation by the State: As seen by the establishment of the SEC and the regulation of financial markets, it signaled a shift toward increased government interference in the economy.

3. Rights of the Worker The Wagner Act ensured that workers could join unions and bargain collectively for better wages and working conditions.

Fourthly, "Infrastructure and Public Works": The New Deal led to considerable improvements in the nation's infrastructure and the creation of jobs through public works programs.

The Democratic Party, under FDR's leadership, shifted its platform to emphasize reform and government intervention, therefore garnering a new and broad constituency.

Disagreements and Criticisms:

Not everyone agreed with the New Deal's policies. It was either overly interventionist or did not go far enough, according to its detractors. Some conservatives and business elites saw it as an unwarranted expansion of government power.

Conclusion:

In guiding the United States through the Great Depression, FDR and the New Deal were crucial. FDR's leadership, together with the breadth of programs and changes that defined the New Deal, had a deep and enduring impact on the nation. The New Deal not only helped individuals in need during the Great Depression, but it also reformed the federal government and set the stage for the modern welfare state and regulatory frameworks.

7.4 The Dust Bowl and the Great Migration: Environmental and Social Disturbances in 1930s America

The 1930s were a difficult time in American history, and two phenomena—the Dust Bowl and the Great Migration—defined this era. These occurrences altered agriculture, population structures, and government policies, all with far-reaching effects on the environment and society as a whole.

The Great Dust Storm:

The Southern Plains of the United States, including significant portions of Texas, Oklahoma, Kansas, Colorado, and New Mexico, were affected by the Dust Bowl. One of the worst environmental disasters in American history occurred in the 1930s as a result of a combination of factors, including a severe drought and unsustainable farming techniques.

Dust Bowl Causes

Over-farming, or 1: The protecting prairie grasses that had prevented soil erosion had been removed as a result of vigorous plowing and cultivation by the farmers.

Drought, 2. Long periods of drought in the region made soil erosion and crop failures even more severe.

3. High Winds: The absence of vegetation combined with strong winds to create large dust storms that blew away the dry, granular earth.

The Dust Bowl's Repercussions:

1) The Collapse of Agriculture: Crop failures and population loss in the farming community were direct results of the Dust Bowl. Thousands of farmers were wiped out economically and had to give up their farms.

As a result of the Dust Bowl and the subsequent Migration, many people left their homes and headed west, with California being a popular destination.

3. Environmental repercussions: Soil erosion, which scarred the land and left it vulnerable to future erosion, was one of the many severe environmental repercussions of the Dust Bowl.

The Government's Reaction (4) In response to the issue, the federal government established the Soil Conservation Service and the Civilian Conservation Corps to enact agricultural policy.

During the Great Migration,

Although the Great Migration began in the early 20th century, it had a profound effect on the 1930s. Millions of African Americans left the rural South for the metropolitan North, Midwest, and West during this massive migration. Economic possibilities, as well as a desire to escape racial discrimination and violence, were primary drivers of the Great Migration.

Factors that Sparked the Great Exodus

1) Economic Opportunities: Industrial Jobs in the North offered higher income and working conditions than their agrarian counterparts in the South.

Discrimination on the basis of race (2): Jim Crow laws, segregation, and racial violence all defined the South. African Americans tried to get away from those kinds of neighborhoods.

3. The Great War African Americans increased in northern cities as a result of the Great Migration and the need for wartime work.

Effects of the Great Exodus:

As a result of Urbanization, African Americans began to make their homes in major cities like Chicago, Detroit, New York, and Los Angeles, where they changed the face of the city and helped establish new, thriving African American neighborhoods.

Contributions to Culture The Great Migration paved the way for the dissemination of new ideas and artistic creations, ultimately giving rise to New York's Harlem Renaissance.

Movement for Civil Rights (3): African Americans in the North and Midwest were exposed to new political and social environments that sparked a desire for civil rights and equality as a result of the Great Migration.

The Dust Bowl's Role in the Great Migration:

The Dust Bowl and the Great Migration may appear unrelated at first glance, but they were actually linked in more ways than one.

In both cases, large numbers of people moved westward. African Americans left the rural South for the urban North and West during the Great Migration, and many Americans fled the Dust Bowl to California in quest of a better life.

(2) The Fight for a Better Future: In both cases, people were moving away from their homes in search of better economic and social conditions. The hope for a better future was what drove the people of the Dust Bowl and the Great Migration.

Changes in society and the population: Both movements altered the population structure and enriched the cultural and social life of the areas they settled in.

Conclusion:

The Great Migration and the Dust Bowl were two of the most significant events of the 1930s in the United States. They caused major shifts in agricultural practices, population dynamics, and cultural production, all of which had far-reaching repercussions on the environment and society. These occurrences demonstrate the fortitude of the American people and their willingness to persevere through difficult times in order to find success.

Chapter 8: World War II and the Postwar Period (1940-1960)

8.1 The United States' Role in World War II: Emerging as a Global Superpower

The United States' participation in World War II marked a watershed moment in the country's development. The United States' transformation from a neutral power to an involved participant in the war profoundly altered the 20th century. World unrest served as a backdrop to the events leading up to and during the war.

The Road to War: Involvement Leading Up to World War II

The United States maintained a position of neutrality and isolationism during the early stages of the war in Europe. The horrors and expenses of World War I left many people reluctant to get involved in another global struggle.

The Lend-Lease Act of 2002 U.S. policy changed in 1941 with the passage of the Lend-Lease Act. It permitted the United States to join the Allied forces by supplying military help to countries fighting against the Axis powers.

Attack on Pearl Harbor, Number Three: The attack on the United States Pacific Fleet at Pearl Harbor, Hawaii, by the Japanese on December 7, 1941, was the defining moment. More than 2,400 Americans were killed in the raid, and it was largely responsible for getting the United States involved in the war.

Mobilization of the U.S. Military and Industrial Bases:

A rapid mobilization of American resources and manpower followed Pearl Harbor. Some of these were:

During World War I, the United States experienced an extraordinary industrial boom as firms moved their focus to the mass manufacturing of weapons, equipment, and supplies. The war effort relied heavily on the nation's industrial might.

As a result of the Selective Service Act of 1940, the number of the United States armed forces was greatly expanded.

Thirdly, Working Women: A large number of women joined the workforce during the war, many of them filling roles that had previously been reserved for men. The influence on traditional gender roles in the United States was profound.

The United States in Europe:

North Africa and Italy: U.S. forces, led by General Dwight D. Eisenhower, were essential in both of these wars. The liberation of Europe from the hands of the Axis powers hinged on the success of these missions.

The D-Day Invasion and Western Europe: The Allied invasion of Normandy on June 6, 1944, widely known as D-Day, represented a critical turning point. The liberation of Western Europe was made possible in large part by the efforts of the United States armed forces during this huge operation.

The Third: The Eastern Front While the U.S. largely fought in Western Europe, the Eastern Front in the Soviet Union was a vital theater of combat against Nazi Germany. The Soviet Union took the biggest hit and made the biggest sacrifices in the war against Nazi Germany.

U.S. Participation in the Pacific War:

Campaign that visits many islands General Douglas MacArthur and Admiral Chester Nimitz led American forces in the Pacific on an island-hopping operation that brought them closer to Japan. Iwo Jima, Midway, and Guadalcanal were also significant engagements.

Hiroshima and Nagasaki, both located in Japan, were hit by atomic bombs delivered by the United States in August of 1945, prompting Japan to surrender. This contentious choice hastened the war's end but will have far-reaching effects on the world.

The United Nations and the Recovery from War:

The United States was instrumental in establishing postwar order as World War II concluded. The most significant changes were:

To encourage international collaboration and forestall future conflicts, the United Nations was founded in 1945. The United States was a driving force behind the formation of the United Nations and a charter member.

Plan Marshall, Number Two: Initiated by the United States, the Marshall Plan provided substantial economic aid to postwar Europe in an effort to repair the continent and forestall the development of communism. The postwar reconstruction phase benefited greatly from this approach.

3. Alliances of World Powers: The United States and the Soviet Union emerged as superpowers in the immediate aftermath of World War II, marking the beginning of the Cold War. To challenge the Soviet Union's sphere of influence, the United States developed alliances like NATO.

Conclusion:

The United States' participation in World War II marked a watershed point in American history, one that ultimately led to the rise of the country to superpower status. From a stance of neutrality to active participation in the war, the United States played a significant role in the defeat of the Axis forces. The United States became a significant participant in reshaping the international order that emerged in the decades following World War II. Both the United States and the rest of the world will forever bear the scars of World War II, which cost millions of lives and had far-reaching effects.

8.2 Discharging Unprecedented Power and Controversy: The Atomic Bomb.

A new level of destructive power was introduced and the path of global politics was altered with the creation and use of the atomic bomb during World War II. There is still much debate on the moral, ethical, and strategic implications of the atomic bomb's development and usage.

What Was the Manhattan Project?

The Manhattan Project, a top-secret research program funded by the United States government during World War II, can be credited with pioneering the development of the atomic bomb. The goal of the project, which began in 1939, was to create an atomic bomb before Nazi Germany. For the difficult mission of developing a workable atomic weapon, it assembled some of the world's best scientists, such as J. Robert Oppenheimer and Enrico Fermi.

The Trinity Check:

New Mexico was the site of the first atomic bomb test, known as "Trinity," on July 16, 1945. The explosion, which was roughly equivalent to 20,000 tons of TNT, proved the viability of nuclear weapons and was a major milestone in the effort.

Hiroshima and Nagasaki:

Hiroshima and Nagasaki were both destroyed by atomic bombs dropped by the United States on Japan on August 6th and 9th, 1945. Radiation exposure from these attacks caused long-term health problems for survivors and other people in the area.

The Ethical and Moral Conundrum:

There were serious ethical and moral concerns brought to light by the dropping of atomic bombs on Hiroshima and Nagasaki. It sparked discussion about whether the attacks were warranted and whether or not such drastic action was necessary. Targeting civilian populations and the concept of noncombatant immunity are still hotly debated.

Thoughts on Strategy

For strategic purposes, dropping an atomic bomb on Japan could have prevented needless casualties that could have resulted from a drawn-out invasion. The attacks were meant to coerce Japan into submission, and they succeeded in doing so.

Nuclear proliferation:

When the atomic bomb was used during WWII, it sparked a nuclear arms race. In 1949, the Soviet Union successfully detonated its first atomic bomb, kicking off decades of rivalry in the race to develop and amass nuclear arsenals. This armaments race defined the Cold War era and dramatically influenced world politics.

Nuclear dissuasion:

The concept of nuclear deterrence emerged when numerous countries acquired nuclear weapons. The concept was that countries wouldn't start global wars because of the risk of annihilation for both sides. This paradigm shaped international relations during the Cold War and remains influential now.

Efforts to Prevent Proliferation

International efforts to stop the spread of nuclear weapons have been made in light of its devastating potential and long-term effects. In 1968, countries signed the Treaty on the Non-Proliferation of Nuclear Weapons (NPT) in an effort to reduce the global nuclear arms race and hasten the process of disarmament.

Nuclear Issues in the 21st Century:

Nuclear terrorism and nuclear war are two of the many problems that the world continues to face because of nuclear weapons. Progress toward disarmament has been gradual despite ongoing efforts to regulate and eliminate nuclear arsenals.

Conclusion:

The atomic bomb, the product of the Manhattan Project and used in the bombings of Hiroshima and Nagasaki, is at once a technological triumph and a moral conundrum. It ended World War II quickly, but it also brought about a new era of global politics and a legacy of destruction. The atomic bomb has had lasting effects on international relations and global security through the nuclear arms race, nuclear deterrence, and the constant fear of nuclear conflict. The debate over the atomic bomb's deployment is a stark reminder of the weight of such extraordinary power.

8.3 The Cold War was a worldwide ideological and power struggle.

Intense geopolitical rivalry and ideological confrontation characterized the world's political environment from the end of World War II until the early 1990s, a time period known as the Cold War. The Cold War had far-reaching effects and left an indelible impression on the 20th century, despite the fact that it never exploded into a direct military confrontation between the United States and the Soviet Union.

The Cold War's Iconic Beginnings

Powerlessness after World War II (1) There was a void of authority in Europe and Asia when Nazi Germany and Imperial Japan were defeated. The United States and the Soviet Union, two rising superpowers, aimed to fill this hole.

Ideological Rivalry (2): The United States, as a symbol of the Western world, has always been a staunch defender of liberalism, free enterprise, and personal autonomy. The Soviet Union, on the other hand, promoted communism, central planning, and a collectivist outlook.

As a result of the occupation of Eastern European countries by the Red Army and the partitioning of postwar Europe (especially Germany), tensions and territorial conflicts arose between the Western and Eastern Blocs.

Important Moments in the Cold War:

Containment: 1. To stop the expansion of communism, the United States implemented a policy of containment, as George F. Kennan notably described in his "Long Telegram." For decades, this strategy was the foundation of U.S. foreign policy.

Marshall Plan and the Truman Doctrine: The Truman Doctrine funded military and economic aid for countries under communist danger. The

European Recovery Program, better known as the Marshall Plan, sought to restore war-ravaged Europe's infrastructure and economy.

Blockade of Berlin and Airlift: After the Soviet Union cut off supplies to West Berlin in 1948, the United States and its allies staged the Berlin Airlift to show their support for West Berlin's independence.

NATO and the Warsaw Pact: The Western nations banded together in 1949 to form the North Atlantic Treaty Organization (NATO), a collective defense alliance. In 1955, the Soviet Union and its Eastern Bloc allies responded by forming the Warsaw Pact.

Fifth, the Korean War The Korean War (1950–1953) was the first armed conflict between the United States and the United Nations and China and the Soviet Union, which were on the side of North Korea.

Space Race, Number Six: Space exploration became a battleground in the Cold War as superpowers raced to be the first to launch artificial satellites like Sputnik and send humans into space like Yuri Gagarin.

The Cuban Missile Crisis, Number Seven The Cuban Missile Crisis of 1962 was the closest the world got to a nuclear war as a result of the Cold War. It was sparked by the Soviet Union's decision to station missiles in Cuba, which led to a tense standoff with the United States.

Vietnam War, Number Eight U.S. involvement in the Vietnam War (1955–1975) was motivated by a desire to stop the spread of communism in Southeast Asia.

Diffused tensions in the 1970s led to arms control agreements and diplomatic endeavors between the two superpowers.

After the Cold War Ended:

The thawing of relations between the superpowers throughout the Cold War culminated with the fall of the Soviet Union in 1991.

To modernize the Soviet system and encourage political and economic change, Mikhail Gorbachev implemented perestroika (restructuring) and glasnost (openness).

2. Revolution in Eastern Europe: People in countries in the region finally spoke up about their yearning for freedom and democracy, which ultimately led to the fall of communist governments.

When the Berlin Wall came down in 1989, it marked the beginning of the end of the Cold War and the end of the separation of Germany.

4. The Fall of the Soviet Union: The Cold War formally ended with the dissolution of the Soviet Union on December 25, 1991.

As a lasting effect of the Cold War,

The Cold War left a lasting impact on international relations:

First, from a "bipolar" to a "unipolar" world: After the Soviet Union collapsed and the Cold War ended, the United States became the only global superpower.

Second, Arms Control and Nuclear Disarmament: Agreements to limit the spread of nuclear weapons and measures to diminish nuclear stockpiles remain vitally critical to maintaining peace and safety around the world.

New security threats have prompted the expansion of NATO and the formation of other alliances and partnerships.

Regional Conflicts, Number Four Regional wars, such as those in Korea, the Middle East, and Ukraine, continue as a result of the Cold War's aftermath.

Economic and ideological factors 5 Capitalism and communism continue to have a role in the political and economic systems of the world, both economically and ideologically.

Despite the absence of open warfare between the superpowers, the Cold War had far-reaching and enduring consequences. It changed the face of international politics, shifted the balance of power, and created a tangled web of lasting strategic alliances, ideological conflicts, and geographical hurdles.

8.4 Economic Growth and the Postwar Baby Boom in the United States

The end of the war, technical advances, and the Baby Boom all contributed to the United States experiencing extraordinary economic success in the decades after World War II. Society, culture, and the United States' place in the global economy all saw radical shifts throughout this time period.

The Economic Boom After World War II:

When WWII finally ended in 1945, a period of unprecedented economic growth began. The United States survived the war relatively undamaged, allowing it to become an economic and industrial superpower. There are a number of important causes that have led to this economic boom:

Demobilization (1) There was demobilization after the war when millions of American troops and women came home. As a result, both the civilian labor force and consumer demand increased rapidly.

Improvements in Technology Significant technological advances had been made throughout the war, particularly in the fields of aircraft, electronics, and medicine. These developments spread to the general public, increasing output and giving rise to new economic sectors.

3. Real Estate Boom: Suburban neighborhoods were up in response to the postwar housing shortage, and millions of new homes were built with assistance from federal programs like the G.I. Bill.

Culture of the Consumer 4 Rising middle-class salaries, innovative new goods, and convenient access to finance all contributed to the development of a consumer society. The rate at which Americans bought things like automobiles, home appliances, and other luxuries increased dramatically.

The Baby Bust:

The Baby Boom was an extremely significant demographic event in the decades after World War II. The "Baby Boom" was the massive uptick in birth rates that started in 1946 and lasted until the middle of the 1960s. There are a number of causes behind this population boom:

Veterans who have recently returned to the country The return of millions of soldiers from World War II created the ideal conditions for families to develop and thrive.

Financial Stability Couples were able to start or expand their families thanks to the booming postwar economy.

Third, the G.I. Bill, which was passed in 1944, made it simpler for veterans to provide for their families by granting them access to low-interest mortgages, educational opportunities, and job training.

4. Cultural Norms: Traditional cultural beliefs encouraged couples to have children by placing a premium on the importance of family and child-rearing.

The Effects of the Recent Baby Boom:

The consequences of the Baby Boom on American culture, politics, and the economy were far-reaching and far-reaching indeed.

1. Population Shift The Baby Boom caused a substantial shift in the age structure of the United States' population, adding a huge and relatively youthful generation.

Second, Economic Development The increased population of young families led to more consumer demand for homes, automobiles, and numerous commodities and services, fueling economic expansion.

Thirdly, an increase in the population meant a greater demand for educational facilities, personnel, and materials.

Fourthly, "Workforce Dynamics" The Baby Boomer generation's entry into the workforce in the 1960s and 1970s was a major factor in shaping both the economy and society at the time.

5. Changes in Culture The civil rights movement, anti-war rallies, and the growth of the counterculture all owe a great deal to the efforts of the Baby Boom generation, who came of age in the 1960s and 1970s.

The Baby Boom's Perplexing Problems

The Baby Boom ushered in a number of positive changes, but it also offered some difficulties.

Education comes first. New schools and more funding were needed to accommodate the soaring number of children entering school in recent decades.

2) Changes in Society and the Economy: The Baby Boomer generation progressed through a wide range of life stages as they matured, from youth to middle age to old age. The difficulties and social effects of each of these changes was different.

Medical Care, Third: The aging Baby Boomers continue to offer issues for the healthcare system, with growing demand for medical services and long-term care as they enter their senior years.

Conclusion:

The United States was profoundly impacted by the Baby Boom that occurred in the decades following World War II. The largest generational cohort in American history was born as a result of favorable economic conditions, cultural beliefs, and government programs. The Baby Boom had far-reaching effects on American culture and society, from economic prosperity and educational opportunities to cultural shifts that are still being felt today.

Chapter 9: Civil Rights and Social Movements (1960-1980)

9.1 Equal rights and justice were central goals of the civil rights movement.

In the United States, the quest of racial equality, social justice, and civil rights for African Americans defined a pivotal and tumultuous time in the middle of the twentieth century known as the Civil Rights Movement. It arose as a reaction to centuries of institutional discrimination, segregation, and racial violence, and it resulted in substantial legislative and societal changes that are still having an effect on the United States today.

Historical Context:

The roots of the Civil Rights Movement may be traced back to the Reconstruction era following the American Civil War. Slavery was ended, citizenship was awarded, and voting rights were expanded for African Americans by the 13th, 14th, and 15th Amendments to the United States Constitution. But these reforms were met with violent opposition in the shape of Jim Crow legislation, racial brutality, and the denial of voting rights.

Civil rights forefathers:

1. NAACP: During the formative years of the Civil Rights Movement, the NAACP, which was established in 1909, was instrumental. It examined how discrimination and segregation are being challenged in court.

Marshall, Thurgood (No. 2): In the NAACP's court cases, notably the seminal Brown v. Board of Education case, the future Supreme Court Justice Thurgood Marshall played a pivotal role.

Rosa Parks, number three: Known as the "mother of the civil rights movement," Rosa Parks gained notoriety in 1955 when she refused to give up her bus seat to a white passenger, which led to the Montgomery Bus Boycott.

Important Steps and Accomplishments:

The Brown v. Board of Education case (1): Brown v. Board of Education, decided in 1954, effectively ended legal segregation in public schools by declaring that state legislation establishing separate public schools for black and white pupils were unconstitutional.

The Montgomery Bus Boycott, Part 2 The Montgomery Bus Boycott was a major event in the movement. It began in 1955 with Rosa Parks' arrest and culminated in a Supreme Court ruling that outlawed racial segregation on public transportation.

Civil Rights Act of 1964, Third: As a watershed piece of legislation, the Civil Rights Act of 1964 made it illegal to treat people differently because of their race, color, religion, sex, or national origin. Numerous facets of American culture were profoundly affected.

Voting Rights Act of 1965, Number Four: The purpose of the Voting Rights Act was to ensure that African Americans and other minorities were able to vote without discrimination. It led to a large increase in voter registration among these populations.

Protest Rally in Washington, D.C. Dr. Martin Luther King Jr. delivered his famous "I Have a Dream" address during the March on Washington for Jobs and Freedom in 1963. He was a staunch supporter of human rights and racial equality.

Members of the Civil Rights Movement Who Made a Huge Impact:

First, Rev. Dr. Martin Luther King, Jr.: Dr. King was a major player in the Civil Rights Movement, conducting countless protests and rallies and promoting civil disobedience as a means to achieve social change.

2. [Malcolm X] Malcolm X was a well-known civil rights leader who pushed for black people to have the right to decide for themselves, be self-reliant, and use force if necessary.

Thirdly, John Lewis: John Lewis was instrumental in the planning and execution of the Selma to Montgomery marches that helped pave the way for the passing of the Voting Rights Act.

Problems & Difficulties:

White supremacist violence, pushback against desegregation, and the glacial pace of change were just a few of the obstacles that the Civil Rights Movement had to overcome. There were disagreements within the movement over strategy and objectives.

History and Persistent Adversity:

Although the Civil Rights Movement won important court cases and ushered in substantial societal transformations, progress toward racial equality remains elusive. Voting rights, criminal justice reform, and institutional racism are all examples of modern problems that show the struggle for civil rights is far from over.

Conclusion:

The Civil Rights Movement was a pivotal time in American history, commemorating a revolutionary period of struggle, sacrifice, and achievement in the drive for racial equality and social justice. It resulted in legislative and social reforms that continue to shape the United States and sparked movements for social justice and equality around the globe.

In the quest of a more just and equitable society, new generations find inspiration in the struggles of the Civil Rights Movement's heroes, in their bravery, and in their dedication to the principles of equality and justice.

9.2 Protests against the Vietnam War and its effects on American society were a divisive time.

From 1955 until 1975, the United States and Vietnam were embroiled in the bloody and contentious Vietnam War, which had lasting effects on both countries. Protests against the war were massive, the country became more politically and culturally divided, and the results had far-reaching effects on American foreign policy.

The Causes and Worsening of the Vietnam War:

The Vietnam War began as a struggle between North Vietnam, headed by communist forces, and South Vietnam, supported by the United States and other anti-communist governments. The policy of containment, which sought to prevent the development of communism, drove the growing U.S. involvement in Vietnam.

First, Colonial Rule by the French French colonial rule over Vietnam from the early to mid-20th century was a major contributing factor to the eventual outbreak of hostilities. The First Indochina War (from 1946 to 1954) was sparked by the fight for independence.

"Geneva Accords" (No. 2) Following the signing of the Geneva Accords in 1954, Vietnam was partitioned along the 17th parallel, with the communist North under Soviet rule and the pro-Western South.

US Involvement (3): The United States began deploying military advisors to South Vietnam in the late 1950s and, under President Lyndon B. Johnson, intensified its military presence, leading to a full-scale American engagement in the battle.

Protests and Opposition to the War:

Protests and opposition against the Vietnam War were a distinguishing aspect of the era in the United States.

To begin with, SDS: [[Students for a Democratic Society]] The Students for a Democratic Society (SDS) was a student activist group that spearheaded anti-war demonstrations, rallies, and teach-ins.

The Draft and the Opposition 2 The draft, which obliged young men to serve in the military, became a focal point of anti-war sentiment. Draft protests, including the burning of draft cards, were prevalent.

Opposition and counterculture, 3. The anti-war rallies of the 1960s were greatly influenced by the counterculture movement, which was characterized by a rejection of established values and standards.

4. Moratorium on the Vietnam War: Millions of Americans struck and demonstrated against the Vietnam War on a national moratorium day in 1969.

5. Shootings at Kent State: In 1970, the shooting of unarmed student protestors by the Ohio National Guard at Kent State University emphasized the intensity of anti-war rallies.

Important People and Groups:

First, Rev. Dr. Martin Luther King, Jr.: Dr. King was a prominent opponent of the war, and he argued that the money being spent on it should be better put to use alleviating poverty and racial inequality at home.

Two words for Muhammad Ali: After refusing to serve in the military due to religious and moral issues, the heavyweight boxing champion became an icon of defiance.

Third, Anti-War Vietnam Veterans These combat veterans formed a group to voice their opposition to the conflict and draw attention to the ethical and moral violations they had seen firsthand.

Effects of Anti-War Demonstrations:

Protests against the war significantly affected public opinion and influenced policymakers:

1) The Views of the People: Public sentiment began to shift against the United States' participation in Vietnam as protests grew more numerous and the conflict dragged on.

New Policies: As part of its Vietnamization program, the Nixon administration began handing over more and more control of the war to its South Vietnamese counterpart.

Third, the war ended in 1973 when the United States withdrew its troops in response to a truce mandated by the Paris Peace Accords. The conflict officially concluded with the fall of Saigon in 1975.

Implications and Lessons:

A significant legacy was left by the Vietnam War and the rallies against it:

First, Social Fractions in the United States: The conflict exacerbated existing differences in American society along generational, political, and cultural lines.

Social activism and political transformation: Many other social movements, such as those for civil rights, women's rights, and environmental protection, can trace their origins to the anti-war era.

Repercussions for American Foreign Policy The Vietnam War influenced U.S. foreign policy decisions and led to heightened legislative monitoring of military actions.

An important part of American history, the Vietnam War and the anti-war rallies that followed it are remembered for the vehement opposition to a divisive conflict and the far-reaching cultural changes they ushered in.

Discussions on war, peace, and the place of dissent in a democracy are all informed by the lessons learnt during this turbulent era.

9.3 Counterculture: The Sixties and the Birth of a New American Culture.

The United States experienced the rise of a significant counterculture throughout the 1960s, which posed serious challenges to established social mores and institutions. This time period, characterized by a cultural revolution led by young people, had far-reaching effects on American culture, politics, and the arts.

History and Origins:

A tangled web of historical, social, and cultural forces gave rise to the counterculture movement of the 1960s:

Prosperity After World War II Many young people in the postwar era had the financial freedom to challenge conventional wisdom and test out new ways of living thanks to the booming economy.

Movement for Civil Rights (2): The fight for civil rights and racial equality in the 1950s and 1960s sparked a wave of action and shook up established power structures.

The Third Vietnam War The anti-war movement in Vietnam galvanized people against the establishment.

Rising access to higher education has produced a new generation of thinkers, researchers, and problem solvers.

Important Aspects of the Counterculture

Several defining characteristics and ideologies distinguished the counterculture:

1. Refusing to Accept Authority The counterculture was an attempt to develop new ways of socializing and expressing oneself that ran opposed to those of the dominant culture.

Two, Anti-Establishment: It posed problems for the state, conventional families, and big business in the United States.

New Ways of Living (3) Members of the counterculture frequently experimented with non-mainstream practices, such as communal living, back-to-the-land movements, and drug use.

4. Anti-War and Civil Rights Movements: Protests and rallies spearheaded by the counterculture helped shape the political climate, opening doors for civil rights activists and those opposed to the war.

Five, Music and Art: Rock 'n' roll and other forms of musical expression, as well as visual art, were crucial to the counterculture movement. Musicians like Bob Dylan, The Beatles, and Andy Warhol achieved legendary status.

The Summer of Love and the Hippies:

Peace, love, and a rejection of consumerism were hallmarks of the counterculture, and the name "hippie" came to be used interchangeably with these ideals. Thousands of young people converged to the Haight-Ashbury district of San Francisco during the "Summer of Love" in 1967 to celebrate countercultural ideas.

Music Festivals, including Woodstock:

The counterculture beliefs and unifying power of music were on full display at music festivals like Woodstock in 1969. Hundreds of thousands of people came together for a weekend of music, peace, and unity at Woodstock.

The counterculture was met with many obstacles and critics.

Repression (1): When authorities responded harshly to counterculture rallies and protests, it often resulted in violence and arrests.

Critique of the Media (2): The mainstream media typically portrayed counterculture adherents as unruly or as threats to society order.

Thirdly, the Fall of Idealism: Due in part to internal disputes and external pressures, the counterculture began to splinter and lose some of its idealism by the late 1960s.

Influence and Lasting Impact:

The counterculture's influence on American culture was far-reaching and long-lasting.

First, Social Movements The counterculture contributed to the greater social and political upheavals of the era, including the civil rights movement, environmental consciousness, and the women's liberation movement.

2. Holistic Health: Interest in holistic health techniques and natural foods emerged as a result of countercultural ideals.

Thirdly, Environmentalism: The present environmental movement can trace its roots back to the counterculture's emphasis on environmental protection.

Technology, number four: The counterculture was essential in the evolution of the personal computer and the internet because of its openness to new ideas and technologies.

Generations of writers, musicians, and visual artists have been influenced by the ideals of the counterculture.

Action over the Long Term(6) Many in the counterculture remained politically and socially active, making strides in areas such as civil rights, LGBTQ+ rights, and social justice.

The counterculture of the 1960s was an important and transformative social movement that altered the trajectory of American history. It showed how effective teenage idealism and social change could be, encouraging the next generation to challenge the status quo and seek a more just and fair society.

9.4 Twin Social Movements of Women's Emancipation and Environmentalism

Women's emancipation and environmental protection were two of the most prominent social movements in the United States in the 1960s and 1970s. Although these movements sought different outcomes, they were united by a commitment to activity and a desire to alter long-standing social conventions and practices.

Feminist movement for women's emancipation:

Second-wave feminism, also known as the Women's Liberation movement, developed in the 1960s in response to the discrimination and inequality that American women experienced at the time. It expanded upon the efforts of first-wave feminists, who in the early 20th century fought for women's suffrage and other fundamental legal rights.

Important Aspects of the Feminist Movement:

 The primary objective of the Women's Liberation movement was to guarantee women's legal equality in all spheres of society, including the home, the classroom, and the job.

Rethinking Traditional Roles: Women started questioning the accepted norms of their gender and fighting for equal rights and less restrictions.

3. Rights to Reproduction Access to contraception and the legal right to have an abortion were important issues in the movement.

The passing of Title IX in 1972, which outlaws sex-based discrimination in education, is a prime example of the work accomplished by women activists in the political sphere.

Literature and Philosophy, No. 5 Authors like Betty Friedan ("The Feminine Mystique") and Gloria Steinem ("Ms. Magazine") emerged as prominent voices in the feminist literary and intellectual canon as a result of the movement.

The Green Movement

Pollution, deforestation, the disappearance of species, and other environmental threats prompted the emergence of the Environmental movement in the United States. An urgent need to save Earth from the consequences of industrialization and human activities propelled the movement.

Priority No. 1: Maintaining and Protecting National parks and clean water supplies were only two examples of the natural areas and resources that the movement fought to protect.

Second, Environmental Legislation: Activists pushed for the adoption of the Clean Air Act, the Clean Water Act, and the establishment of the Environmental Protection Agency (EPA).

Earth Day (Nov. 3) Millions of people around the United States showed their support for environmental causes on the first Earth Day, which was held on April 22, 1970.

Efforts to Reduce Pollution (4) The environmental movement has successfully pressured polluting businesses to adopt more eco-friendly processes and equipment.

5. Conservation Groups Many groups, like the Sierra Club and the Natural Resources Defense Council, were instrumental in advancing environmental protection.

Intersectionality and Common Objectives:

There was a lot of overlap between the Women's Liberation and Environmental movements. Many women who engaged in Women's Liberation were also passionate about environmental issues. Similar goals of challenging existing power systems and promoting a more equal and sustainable future united the two groups.

Legacy and Persistent Difficulties:

Major victories were won by both movements:

1. The Feminist Movement: The advancement of women in both academia and the workforce may be directly attributed to the efforts of the Women's Liberation movement. There has been some success in the fight for women's rights, but there is still a long way to go.

The Environmental Movement The Environmental movement was instrumental in shifting public opinion and government policy toward the environment. New issues, such as global warming and biodiversity loss, are still being tackled today.

Both movements stress the importance of social and environmental justice, pushing for a world that is more egalitarian and sustainable. They are evidence of the efficacy of activism and the potential for positive change when people band together to combat the current quo and create a brighter future.

Chapter 10: Contemporary America (1980-Present)

10.1 A Watershed Moment in American Politics, the Reagan Years and the Rise of the Conservative Movement

The Reagan Era, represented by the administration of Ronald Reagan from 1981 to 1989, marked a crucial turning point in American politics. There was a revival of conservatives during this time, which had a profound impact on the country's economic policies, diplomatic relations, and domestic objectives.

The Conservative Renewal's Historic Roots

Multiple causes contributed to the right's comeback during Reagan's presidency.

1) Dissatisfaction with the Government: Stagnant economies, high inflation, and widespread disenchantment with government were hallmarks of the 1970s. Loss of faith in government was exacerbated by Watergate and the Vietnam War.

(2) Conservative Ideology: A burgeoning conservative movement, bolstered by the ideas of people like William F. Buckley Jr. and the growth of the New Right, pushed for smaller government, personal freedom, and preservation of traditional morals and ethics.

(3) Reagan's Argument Former California governor Ronald Reagan emerged as a charismatic figure who could bring together conservatives of many stripes and strike a chord with people.

Some Highlights from the Reagan Years:

Several prominent traits and policy movements defined the Reagan administration:

1. Economic Policies: Commonly referred to as "Reaganomics," Reagan's economic policies centered on supply-side economics and featured considerable tax cuts. The goals of these measures were to increase economic activity and decrease inflation.

Reagan supported deregulation in the financial sector, the aviation industry, and the trucking industry to boost competition and decrease government intrusion.

Third, Reagan pushed for a massive military expansion, with an accompanying rise in defense budget, to fortify national defense and project American preeminence in the Cold War.

The Reagan administration was quite tough on the Soviet Union, labeling it a "evil empire" and using containment and pressure as its main tactics.

5. Anti-Communism: Reagan aided anti-Soviet troops in Afghanistan and Nicaragua and supported anti-communist initiatives in other nations.

War on Drugs, Number Six: During the Reagan administration, stricter drug legislation and intensified law enforcement operations were implemented to combat drug usage and trafficking.

Social Conservatism: The Reagan administration shared the beliefs of social conservatives, such as those who are against abortion and in favor of "family values."

Impediments and Rebuttals:

Reagan was well-liked by conservative voters, yet his policies and conduct were challenged.

1 - Economic Disparity There were others who felt that the wealthiest were favored and that income inequality rose as a result of Reaganomics.

Second, Environmental Concerns arose because of the deregulation initiatives, which had an effect on the environment and public health.

Third, Debt and Deficiencies: Budget deficits and the national debt both increased under Reagan's economic policies, despite his tax cuts.

The Reagan administration's involvement in the Iran-Contra controversy, in which funds from the sale of arms to Iran were used to support anti-Sandinista guerrillas in Nicaragua, threw a pall over Reagan's presidency.

Influence and Lasting Impact:

The Reagan administration changed American politics forever.

First, the Conservative Movement saw its influence inside the Republican Party grow and become more stable during Reagan's presidency.

Second, Economic Measures: The Republican Party was forever changed by Reagan's economic policies, which pushed for lower taxes, less regulation, and less government involvement in the market.

Thirdly, the End of the Cold War is credited to Reagan's combative approach toward the Soviet Union.

Social conservatism, number four: The Republican Party's platform and policy ideas are heavily influenced by the social conservatism of the Reagan era.

Nationalism: National identity and pride: Reagan's emphasis on American exceptionalism and national pride: These ideas still reverberate in contemporary American politics.

A new conservative worldview and different economic and foreign policies defined the Reagan Era, which was a watershed moment in American history. Reaganomics and the conservative movement remain important to the platform of the Republican Party, which means it continues to impact the political scene today. The impact of Ronald Reagan's administration is multifaceted and controversial, even today in American politics.

10.2 The Rise of Technology and its Impact on Society

A time of rapid and deep change in the ways in which people, corporations, and society function, the technological revolution is also known as the digital or information age. The proliferation of internet use and other forms of digital communication, as well as the increasing pervasiveness of digital gadgets, are defining features of this revolution.

Evolution and Prehistory:

The advent of computers and the internet in the middle of the twentieth century marked the beginning of the technological revolution. Some major checkpoints are:

First, the Microchip was Invented. The microchip, invented in the '50s, allowed for the downsizing of electronic components, leading to the development of more compact and powerful computers.

2. The Development of the Internet Digital communication networks owe a great deal to the ARPANET, an early version of the internet that was developed in the late 1960s.

The widespread availability of computing was facilitated by the development of personal computers in the 1970s and 1980s. Examples of these machines are the Apple II and the IBM PC.

Tim Berners-Lee's invention of the World Wide Web in 1989 radically altered the nature of online information dissemination and consumption.

5. Mobile Devices: Since the introduction of the first iPhone in 2007, mobile devices have proliferated, ushering in the age of smartphones and constant online access.

Among the most notable aspects of the technological revolution are:

Several distinguishing characteristics define the technological revolution:

The Digital Shift, #1: It triggered a transition from analog to digital technology, which has repercussions across many sectors, including media, business, and transportation.

The internet and other forms of digital communication have brought individuals from all over the world together and expanded the reach of knowledge and resources.

Thirdly, an excessive amount of data: Information overload is a result of the internet's wealth of data, necessitating sophisticated search and filtering tools.

4. Automation and Artificial Intelligence: Recent developments in robotics, machine learning, and AI have altered traditional methods of labor and prompted concerns about the future of some occupations.

5. Online Shopping and E-Commerce The rise of e-commerce platforms, led by Amazon and eBay, has completely altered the retail industry.

6. Networking and Social Media The proliferation of social media has completely altered the dynamics of interpersonal and business relationships.

Effects on Culture:

The advent of modern technology has caused widespread societal changes:

Communication is the first. Email, social media, and video conferencing are just some of the digital innovations that have made it possible to instantly communicate with individuals all over the world.

2. Business and Work: Companies have embraced the digital age, with telecommuting, online shopping, and data-driven decisions replacing traditional methods of doing business as the standard.

3. Education: Online education platforms and digital resources have revolutionized how people obtain knowledge and training.

Streaming services, online gaming, and the ability to make original content digitally have all had a major impact on the entertainment business in the past few years.

Healthcare 5. Digital Health Technologies: Digital Health Technologies, Telemedicine, and Wearable Devices have enhanced healthcare access and patient outcomes.

6. Privacy and Security: Data privacy, cybersecurity, and monitoring are now widely recognized as pressing challenges in modern society.

Issues of Concern and Difficulty:

Despite its many positive effects, the technology revolution has also given rise to serious problems:

Inequalities in access to technology and the internet continue to widen, resulting in a "digital divide" that has repercussions for students' success in the classroom, their ability to find work, and their ability to learn new material.

Security and Privacy Concerns over personal privacy have been exacerbated by internet firms' acquisition and use of customer data, while the ever-present danger of cyberattacks has thrust the topic of cybersecurity into the spotlight.

3. Job Displacement: Automation and artificial intelligence have the potential to displace specific jobs and require worker adaptability.

Fourthly, Manipulation of Information The proliferation of false information and propaganda on the internet has prompted serious questions regarding the veracity of data posted on the web.

Directions for the Future:

Emerging technologies such as 5G, virtual reality, and the Internet of Things (IoT) are determining the future of the ongoing technological revolution. Smart cities, autonomous vehicles, and tailored medicine are just a few examples of how technology is being integrated into everyday life and promising to bring about additional revolutionary change.

In sum, the technology revolution has altered our culture, economics, and methods of engagement with the outside world. Technology brings both obstacles and opportunities, and it is important to find a middle ground between advancing the state of the art and sacrificing fundamental rights and freedoms like privacy, safety, and fairness. Even if the future will be shaped in ways that are hard to foresee, the current digital transformation gives hope for positive change and advancement in a wide range of disciplines.

10.3 Watershed Moment in American History, 9/11 and the War on Terror

The 9/11 terrorist attacks, also known as "9/11," were a sad and life-altering event that changed the United States and the globe forever. These assaults, carried out by the extremist group al-Qaeda, led to a fundamental shift in U.S. foreign policy and the commencement of the War on Terror, a global campaign against terrorism.

The Attacks on September 11:

In the early hours of September 11, 2001, 19 al-Qaeda members hijacked four passenger jets. The World Trade Center in New York City was destroyed when two of these planes were deliberately flown into the twin towers. United Flight 93 crashed in a Pennsylvania field after passengers attempted to regain control from the hijackers, and a second plane slammed into the Pentagon in Arlington, Virginia.

Important Reactions and Outcomes:

First and foremost, there was a tremendous loss of life on 9/11, making it the greatest terrorist act in human history.

People from all walks of life came together to show their support for the victims and their families after the assaults, and the nation as a whole was shaken to its core.

U.S. Rebuttal No. 3 The United States promptly started Operation Enduring Freedom in Afghanistan to root out al-Qaeda and topple the Taliban government that had protected the terrorist organization.

The Fourth Reason for Establishing the Department of Homeland Security After 9/11, the United States created the Department of Homeland Security to better coordinate anti-terrorist activities.

Patriot Act, number five: Concerns about civil liberties and privacy arose when the USA PATRIOT Act was passed in October 2001, giving law enforcement agencies wide powers to combat terrorism.

The Fight Against Terror

In response to 9/11, the world has been engaged in a global war against terrorism. Important features of this campaign were:

In addition to its involvement in Afghanistan's conflict, the United States spearheaded a coalition invasion of Iraq in 2003 to topple Saddam Hussein over concerns over his country's stockpile of WMD. A lot of people have strong feelings on the Iraq war.

Operations Against Terrorism The United States and its allies conducted counterterrorism operations all over the world, primarily focusing on the al-Qaeda network. Drones and special troops were important in these endeavors.

U.S. authorities have taken extra precautions and increased information sharing in an effort to forestall further terrorist assaults on American territory.

Problems and Disagreements:

The War on Terror was fraught with difficulties and debates:

First, Civilian Casualties: Ethical and legal concerns were raised due to civilian deaths caused by military activities and counterterrorism operations.

Detention facility in Guantanamo Bay: Guantanamo Bay, where terrorism suspects were being imprisoned without trial, sparked widespread outcry and legal challenges around the world.

3. Methods of Torture and Interrogation: The use of advanced interrogation tactics, like as waterboarding, which many people view as torture, caused a lot of controversy.

4. Diminished Freedoms Civil liberties and the right to privacy were a source of worry as a result of the War on Terror, especially in light of the increased surveillance of citizens.

Legacy and Persistent Difficulties:

The effects of 9/11 and the War on Terror on the United States and the rest of the world will be felt for a long time to come.

Alterations in the geopolitical order Conflicts and realignments in the Middle East and abroad have their roots in the War on Terror, which fundamentally altered U.S. foreign policy and the country's place in the globe.

Safety and Monitoring Since 9/11, discussions of national security and surveillance have dominated discussions about individual liberty.

Thirdly, PTSD in Veterans: Long-term effects on veterans and their families are felt from the high rates of post-traumatic stress disorder (PTSD) and physical injuries among U.S. military personnel as a result of the conflicts in Afghanistan and Iraq.

4. Continued Danger Despite the fact that we have achieved great strides against al-Qaeda, we are still facing a global threat from terrorism due to the rise of new extremist groups and lone-wolf assaults.

The 9/11 attacks and the subsequent War on Terror are a watershed point in American history, with far-reaching repercussions that are still felt today. The nation's response to these events demonstrates both the strength of the American people and the difficulty of striking a balance between security and civil freedoms.

10.4 The Political and Social Landscape in the 21st Century

Changes in politics and society have had a significant impact on the world in the 21st century. The world we live in has been profoundly impacted by the events of this age, from the advent of new technology and the perils of climate change to the evolution of political ideologies and the modification of societal standards.

Advances in Technology:

One of the defining elements of the 21st century has been the rapid growth of technology. Important changes include:

1) The Web and social media: The proliferation of internet use and the popularity of social media sites have fundamentally altered human interaction, knowledge sharing, and political debate.

Phones with Internet access on the go (2): The widespread availability of smartphones and other mobile devices has made it possible to be in constant contact with loved ones no matter where they may be.

Third, Artificial Intelligence: AI developments have influenced the automation, machine learning, and data analysis businesses, as well as the labor market.

4. E-commerce: E-commerce platforms and online purchasing have altered the retail industry and the way consumers make purchases.

Environmental Worries and the Impact of Climate Change:

Climate change and environmental issues have become important worldwide concerns. In the 21st century, people have become more aware of climate change and have taken steps to combat it.

The Paris Accord 1. In 2015, world leaders signed the Paris Agreement to reduce greenhouse gas emissions and adapt to the repercussions of climate change.

2. Renewable Energy: Concerns about carbon emissions and the need for sustainable energy have accelerated the shift toward renewable energy sources like solar and wind power.

The Third Wave of Environmental Protest: Greta Thunberg and the Fridays for Future movement are just two examples of the new generation of environmental activists that have propelled climate change to the forefront of international discussions.

Shifts in Politics:

There have been several noteworthy political changes and advancements in the 21st century, including:

The Growth of Populism 1. In many nations, populist individuals and movements have risen to prominence, posing a threat to long-standing political and institutional order.

Changes in the balance of power in the world, such as China's emergence as a global power, have reworked the foundations of international politics.

3. Evolving Alliances: Traditional alliances, such as NATO, have adapted to shifting geopolitical conditions, while new regional and bilateral partnerships have arisen.

4. Global Health Challenges: The 2019 COVID-19 pandemic put international cooperation and governance to the test and revealed flaws in the world's healthcare systems.

Evolution in Society:

The 21st century has seen a dramatic shift in social mores and values:

1) Equal Rights in Marriage Many countries, including the United States in 2015, took a major step toward broader LGBTQ+ rights and acceptance when they legalized same-sex marriage.

Second, Empowerment of Women: Because of the #MeToo movement and other advocacy activities, more people are talking about gender equality now than ever before.

Thirdly, Immigration and Migration: Many countries' immigration policy, refugee crises, and multiculturalism have all been questioned as a result of people crossing borders.

To combat systematic racism and police violence, protests and social justice movements, such as Black Lives Matter, have emerged.

Medical Care and Epidemics:

Public health and healthcare have received a lot of focus in the 21st century.

To increase access and lessen inequalities, many nations, notably the United States with the Affordable Care Act, have undertaken healthcare reforms.

Second, pandemics Pandemic readiness and worldwide collaboration in health care are more important than ever in the wake of the appearance of new infectious diseases like SARS, Ebola, and COVID-19.

The potential and difficulties of the 21st century are equal.

Income inequality, social inequities, and varying levels of healthcare and educational opportunity are all issues that need to be addressed.

Cybersecurity, secondly: Increased cyber risks and difficulties are a result of our ever-increasing reliance on digital technologies.

Third, Demographic Changes: The effects of an aging population and other demographic shifts on labor markets, social services, and economy in many countries.

4. Knowledge and Abilities: Constant difficulties exist in educating people to meet the demands of a dynamic labor market and a technologically advanced era.

As the 21st century progresses, people all around the world will be working to solve these intricate problems and figure out how to best manage the intricate web of connections between technology, politics, society, and the environment. To meet the obstacles and seize the opportunities of this century, one must be flexible, cooperative, and creative.

Conclusion

A. The United States as a Superpower

The United States is a global powerhouse in all spheres of international influence, including economics, politics, and the military. For the better part of the twentieth century and into the twenty-first, the United States has been a superpower. The United States' economic might, military prowess, cultural impact, and global diplomatic involvement all contribute to the country's status as a superpower.

Influence in the Market

A strong and varied economy is a key factor in the United States' ability to maintain its standing as a global superpower. Fundamental features consist of:

1) The World's Biggest Economy The United States has the highest nominal GDP in the world thanks to its thriving private sector, constant innovation, and talented workforce.

(2) International Trade With its substantial position in global financial institutions and vast economic linkages to other countries, the United States is a key player in global trade.

When it comes to technical innovation and research, the United States is unrivaled, with Silicon Valley and other tech hubs serving as global centers of excellence.

4. Cultural Exports: American pop culture has a profound impact on international aesthetics and trends, from film and television to music and fashion.

A key component of the United States' reputation as a global powerhouse is the strength of its military.

1. Budget for Defense: The United States has the largest defense budget in the world, allowing for the continuous improvement and growth of its military.

(2) Nuclear Arms: The United States' nuclear arsenal is both a deterrent to its enemies and an important part of international efforts to limit nuclear weapons.

Worldwide Exposure 3. The United States maintains a sizable military presence and rapid reaction capacity because to its many bases and forces stationed in strategic locations across the world.

The United States strengthens its military influence and cooperation through its alliances with various countries.

Soft power and diplomacy:

As a permanent member of the United Nations Security Council and through its extensive system of embassies and consulates, the United States engages in diplomacy.

Soft power (1) The United States uses its cultural influence, educational system, and foreign assistance programs to further its interests around the world.

Foreign Assistance (2): The United States is one of the world's largest donors, providing aid for things like international development, humanitarian aid, and disaster relief.

Thirdly, Trade Agreements: The United States plays a pivotal role in defining international economic and political order through its participation in international institutions and the negotiation of trade agreements.

The Obstacles and Obligations:

The United States, as a global superpower, must deal with special pressures and responsibilities.

World Safety (1) The U.S. is often called upon to confront and settle global conflicts, act in humanitarian situations, and counter terrorism.

Financial Management 2. The United States' contributions to international monetary stability, economic expansion, and the resolution of financial crises are taken for granted.

Thirdly, Climate Change The United States, as a significant contributor to global carbon emissions, must take action to mitigate climate change and other environmental threats.

4. Leadership in Humanitarian Action In times of catastrophe, the United States is often looked to as a role model for its humanitarian aid efforts.

Complicated International Relations:

The United States' position as a global superpower makes international relations more complicated.

The United States has the difficulty of navigating competing agendas among its friends as it seeks to advance its own national interests and retain its partnerships.

Rising countries like China and Russia pit the United States against one another, creating global competition and nuanced dynamics.

Terrorism, cyberthreats, and public health crises are all examples of transnational issues that call for the coordinated efforts of world leaders.

Continuous Function:

The United States' role as a superpower remains crucial in the 21st century. The United States remains a major player in shaping and influencing the international order through its efforts to address global concerns, negotiate trade agreements, promote human rights, and respond to disasters. The United States is a pivotal player in a dynamic global scene because its superpower status reflects both its power and its responsibility.

B. Persistent Problems and Prospects in the 21st Century

The problems and opportunities that face humanity in the twenty-first century are as varied as they are complex. There are many interconnected problems that need creative solutions and international cooperation as communities, economies, and governments adjust to rapid technological, environmental, and geopolitical changes. In this article, we look at how several current issues and potential future developments are impacting the current environment.

First, Environmental Permanence in the Face of Climate Change:

Climate change is a serious threat to ecosystems, businesses, and people's way of life, and addressing it is a significant challenge. Rising global temperatures, catastrophic weather events, and sea-level rise are just a few of the impacts. In order to tackle this issue, the international community will need to work together to cut emissions of greenhouse gases.

Opportunity: The shift to a low-carbon, sustainable economy offers the chance to increase innovation, the number of available jobs, and environmental protection. Opportunities for investment are particularly promising in the areas of renewable energy, energy efficiency, and green technologies.

(2) Cybersecurity and Technology:

The rapid development of technology has increased people's susceptibility to cyberattacks, data breaches, and privacy invasions, posing a significant challenge. Governments and businesses must now prioritize the protection of vital infrastructure and personal data.

Opportunity: The technology industry presents possibilities for societal development, technological advancement, and service enhancement. Cybersecurity, AI, and digital communication innovations may one day revolutionize entire industries while also making them safer places to work.

The pandemic of COVID-19 has underlined the significance of preparedness and international cooperation in the face of health disasters, while also exposing flaws in global healthcare systems.

This difficulty might be viewed as an opportunity to improve healthcare systems, advance medical research, and forge stronger international public health organizations.

4. Poverty and Economic Disparity:

Problem: Inequality of wealth persists as a global and domestic issue. There is a serious lack of parity in terms of access to resources like schools, hospitals, and jobs.

Growth in the economy, progressive social policies, and ethical business practices all have the potential to lessen economic disparity and the severity of poverty. Inclusionary economic growth can be fostered by investments in people's education and employability.

5. Conflict and tension in international relations:

Challenge: Instability and tension are exacerbated by geopolitical rivalry, regional conflicts, and competing interests among global powers. These concerns challenge peace and international collaboration.

Opportunity: Diplomacy, conflict resolution, and international collaboration offer ways to lessen the severity of conflicts, find areas of agreement, and tackle problems that affect everyone. The United Nations and other multilateral organizations are instrumental in these pursuits.

6. Shifts in the Demographic Makeup:

Problem: Workforce dynamics, healthcare, and social services face issues in regions with both aging and expanding youth populations.

Opportunity: Addressing demographic concerns and contributing to economic and social well-being through a diversified workforce, intergenerational collaboration, and innovative solutions in healthcare and social services.

Education and Skill Acquisition, Number Seven:

Preparing people for the ever-evolving labor market and giving them the tools they'll need to succeed in the digital age is a constant problem.

Opportunity: In today's competitive job market, investing in one's education and skill set, including digital literacy and vocational training, can give one a leg up.

The pursuit for equality and justice is hampered by the persistence of discrimination, human rights abuses, and social inequities in many regions of the world.

Opportunities to solve these difficulties and advance human rights, social justice, and equality for everyone can be found in grassroots movements, legal reforms, and international organizations.

9. Biodiversity and Environmental Stability:

Threatening ecosystems, animals, and international peace and security is the loss of biodiversity and the unsustainable consumption of natural resources.

There is a window of opportunity to preserve biodiversity and guarantee Earth's well-being through sustainable land management, conservation activities, and international accords.

Tenth, Migration and Refugee Disasters:

Challenge: Large refugee and migration crises have resulted from people being uprooted from their homes owing to war, persecution, or the natural environment.

Opportunity: International cooperation, refugee integration programs, and humanitarian aid can help displaced people right away and pave the way for more permanent solutions to their problems.

It is becoming increasingly apparent that a holistic and multidisciplinary strategy is necessary in order to solve these difficulties and seize these opportunities. Sustainable, fair, and generationally beneficial solutions can only be found when governments, organizations, and individuals work together on local, regional, and global stages. The 21st century, with all its complications, offers a rare chance to solve global problems and build a better, more equitable, and environmentally sustainable world.

C. Tapestry of Diversity and Complexity: Reflections on the American Experience

History, culture, politics, and the individual experiences of the American people all come together to form a complex tapestry. It's been an up-and-down road full of lessons, and it's still changing to represent the dynamic interplay of principles, values, and obstacles. The relevance of the American experience is discussed, along with some of its major elements.

Groundwork in the Past:

Beginning with the entrance of European settlers in the 17th century and the founding of the 13 colonies, the American experience has profound historical roots. The history of the United States is a sequence of defining episodes that continue to form its identity, from the fight for independence and the drafting of the U.S. Constitution to westward expansion and the Civil War.

Differences and Newcomers:

Diversity is intrinsic to the United States' very essence. Immigrants from all walks of life and all corners of the globe have enriched the cultural tapestry of this country over the course of its history. The American experience is a reflection of the multiplicity of voices, traditions, and perspectives that have come together to construct a shared narrative.

The Struggle for Liberty and Equality:

Freedom and equality are entwined with the American experience. Because of Thomas Jefferson's declaration that "all men are created equal" in the Declaration of Independence, oppressed groups including women, African Americans, Native Americans, and the LGBTQ+ community have had to fight for equality and freedom ever since.

The Spirit of Innovation:

The American experience is distinguished by an innovative attitude that has led to unprecedented developments in technology, industry, and science. The American spirit of innovation has shaped the world we live in, from the Industrial Revolution to the Information Age.

Problems and Social Fairness:

The American story also had to deal with serious difficulties. Racism, economic inequality, and social justice gaps are just a few of the problems that the United States has had to face. The battle for equality and justice is reflected in historical movements such as the Civil Rights Movement, the Women's Suffrage Movement, and the Black Lives Matter Movement.

Democratic Participation and Active Citizenship:

Democracy and active participation in one's community are cornerstones of the American experience. Elections, advocacy, and activism all play crucial roles in molding the course of a nation, and citizens have the right to take part in these processes.

The American story isn't limited to the United States. The United States' foreign policy and diplomatic initiatives have a significant impact on global events, from wars to the fight against climate change.

Continuous Introspection and Modification:

The American story is never finished. It exemplifies the United States' flexibility in the face of adversity, its willingness to improve upon its flaws, and its pursuit of a more ideal union. When we look back on the American experience, we must accept that there was room for improvement and that change is a process, not a destination.

Common Goals and Ideals

Although the American experience is rich and varied, there are common ideals and goals that bind the country together. Freedom, equality before the law, a respect for individual rights, and the opportunity to pursue one's own happiness are all recurring themes in the history of the United States.

Inclusion and mutual respect

Unity in variety is a defining feature of the American experience. It is a monument to the strength of the American ideal that the country has been able to unite people of such different origins beneath a common flag. It symbolizes the country's fortitude and ability to recover from adversity.

Affect on a Global Scale:

The American experience is not confined to the nation's borders. It has a profound impact on worldwide thought and culture, politics, and the economy.

In conclusion, the American story is dynamic and varied, and it is constantly developing. It's an inspiring tale of overcoming adversity. The American experience is a reflection of a nation that is constantly working toward a more equitable and prosperous tomorrow. It's motivational because it symbolizes the never-ending search for liberty, equality, and prosperity that all humans share.